HOW TO
SHARPEN
ANYTHING

HOW TO SHARPEN ANYTHING

BY DON GEARY

TAB BOOKS Inc.
BLUE RIDGE SUMMIT, PA. 17214

FIRST EDITION
FIRST PRINTING

Copyright © 1983 by TAB BOOKS Inc.
Printed in the United States of America

Reproduction or publication of the content in any manner, without express
permission of the publisher, is prohibited. No liability is assumed with respect to
the use of the information herein.

Library of Congress Cataloging in Publication Data

Geary Don.
How to sharpen anything.

Includes index.
1. Sharpening of tools. I. Title.
TJ1280.G33   1983   621.9′   82-5955
ISBN 0-8306-2463-5   AACR2
ISBN 0-8306-1463-X (pbk.)

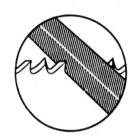

Contents

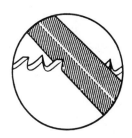

Introduction

Almost any tool that you may use will have a cutting or working edge and for the tool to work efficiently, this edge must be maintained. A dull knife, for example, is just about useless when a cutting task is at hand, but a sharp knife will slice through the work with little effort on the user's part. Based on the theory that a sharp tool is the only type to use, this book takes a look at almost every tool that requires maintenance of a cutting edge. Here you will find solid information about how a cutting edge is developed (in the event that the original edge was damaged) as well as how to sharpen tools that just aren't cutting well because they are dull. In addition to common edged tools—knives, saw chains, and wood chisels—you will also learn about other tools that will work much more effectively if they are sharpened—can openers, rakes, shovels, and wrenches.

We begin with a look at the tools that are used for sharpening—grinding wheels, files, and sharpening stones as well as the best types of lubrication to use while sharpening. By the end of that chapter you will have a strong basis for choosing a sharpening tool for any sharpening task.

The rest of the book explains how to sharpen a wide variety of tools, and these are grouped according to categories. A quick glance at the Table of Contents should lead you to the chapter that explains how to sharpen a given tool. For example, if you want information about how to sharpen a plane, you will find this in Chapter 3 on Hand Woodworking Tools.

Miscellaneous Sharpening is a catch-all chapter for many tools that are often neglected when it comes to sharpening but that will nevertheless benefit from some type of edge treatment. The household can opener is just one example of the type of tool discussed.

This book is designed to show you how to sharpen almost any tool you may own or use, and it should be consulted before sharpening is attempted. Although there is nothing particularly difficult about sharpening in general, there is usually a special angle or sharpening technique that spells the difference between success and failure. I have tried to include such information wherever possible to aid you in sharpening common (and not-so-common) tools around the home and workshop. This information, coupled with a conscientious approach, will enable you to sharpen any given tool. After all is said and done, a sharp tool is a safe tool that will help you to accomplish a given task quickly and with predictable results.

Chapter 1

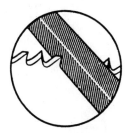

Sharpening Tools

While it is entirely possible to put an edge on a tool with a rock from the garden (Fig. 1-1), you will fins sharpening much easier to accomplish if you choose the right type of sharpening tool for the task at hand. This can be somewhat confusing when you consider that there are probably *hundreds* of different sharpening tools available. The list includes a wide variety of sharpening stones, files, abrasive papers, sharpening steels, and grinding wheels. Add to this the number of sharpening aids, guides, electronic devices, and other "gizmos" available, and it is easy to understand why the average person has no idea of just what the "right" sharpening tool for a particular task may be. In this chapter we look at sharpening tools and explain the use of each. In the end you should have a clear understanding of which sharpening tool to choose for every sharpening task.

SHARPENING STONES

There are many types, shapes and sizes of sharpening stones available, and undoubtedly there are several good choices for almost any sharpening project. In general, all sharpening stones fall into one of two rather large groups: *natural* and *man-made* sharpening stones.

Natural sharpening stones are, as the name suggests, stones that are found in nature. Some of the more familiar ones include *emery* (which has probably been used for the longest period of time), *garnet, quartz*, and several blue stone abrasives, which are found in the states of Arkansas and Ohio. Later in this chapter we will discuss the more popular of these natural stones in detail.

Man-made sharpening stones are generally harder than natural sharpening stones (except of course for diamond dust abrasives,

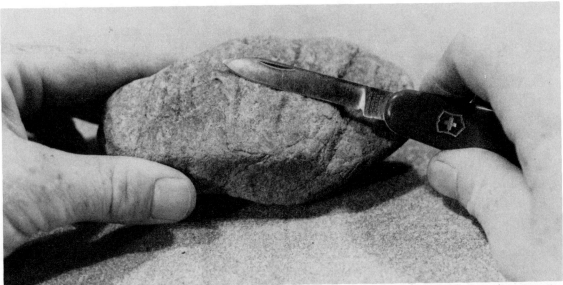

Fig. 1-1. While a knife can be sharpened with a rock, you will do a much better job of sharpening with a stone that is made for the purpose.

which are the hardest of all abrasives). In addition, man-made sharpening stones are uniform in grit size. This small fact may not seem very important at first, but having uniform grit throughout a sharpening stone makes predictable sharpening possible. It should be noted at this point that natural sharpening stones do not have this degree of uniformity. For this reason, man-made stones are preferable for most sharpening tasks.

All man-made sharpening stones are composed of two basic parts: the *abrasive*, and a *bonding agent* which holds the grains of abrasive in a usable form (such as a sharpening stone or grinding wheel). Each of these parts is equally important.

ABRASIVES

The abrasive grains in a sharpening stone (and grinding wheels as well) are the elements that actually perform the cutting during the sharpening process. During a sharpening operation, each of these grains fracture, resulting in a new cutting surface or edge. This means that there is an almost continual rejuvenation of the sharpening stone's surface, ensuring that the stone is accomplishing the sharpening task as best it can. Eventually, individual grains of abrasive fracture to the point where they can no longer cut. When this happens, the adhesive releases its hold and the useless grain of abrasive is allowed to float free on the surface where it is carried away by the oil used during the sharpening. This is an ongoing process, and abrasive particles from below take over the cutting or sharpening. Since all man-made sharpening stones are composed of millions of abrasive particles, you can reasonably expect such a stone to perform well for a long period of time.

It is now possible to manufacture man-made sharpening stones in an almost infinite variety of abrasive grain size and type. The larger the abrasive grain size, the faster it will cut or remove metal from a cutting edge, but this will also result in a rough texture on the metal being sharpened. Fine abrasive grit sizes remove less material and result in a metal surface that is much smoother to the point of polishing rather than actually removing much metal from the tool being sharpened (Fig. 1-2).

After the material has been crushed, it is passed through a series of screens to sort it by size. The ultimate grit size is determined by the number of meshes per linear inch in the screen used to separate the various grains. Finer grit sizes are separated by hydraulic or air classification methods. Sizes of grit range from 4 o 1000 with the coarse grains having the lower number.

There are a number of different abrasive grainlike materials currently used to make sharpening stones and grinding wheels.

Aluminum Oxide

Aluminum oxide is a manufactured abrasive produced by fusing bauxite in an electric furnace at a temperature of about 3700 degrees Fahrenheit. During a typical run, fresh supplies of bauxite are added to the furnace continually. The finished product is a large "pig" of crystalline aluminum oxide which is then broken up, crushed, and sized to various usable grain sizes. This sizing is done by passing the pulverized aluminum oxide abrasive grains through various sizes of mesh screening which effectively separates the grain according to size. Aluminum oxide abrasive is a tough,

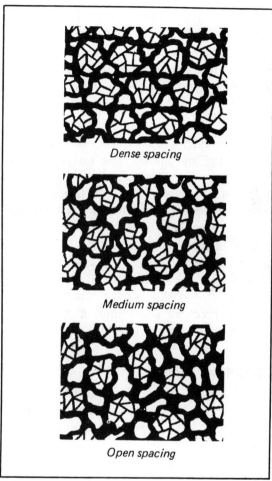

Dense spacing

Medium spacing

Open spacing

Fig. 1-2. The grain spacing of a sharpening stone will determine the cutting speed.

sharp grain bearing the chemical formula AL203.

Silicon Carbide

Silicon carbide abrasive is made by converting pure silica sand and petroleum coke into silicon carbide in a resistant-type electric furnace at around 4000 degrees Fahrenheit.

3

After cooling, the resulting mass is broken up, carefully sorted, crushed, and sized to a usable range of grit sizes. Silicon carbide is harder and sharper than aluminum oxide. The chemical formula for silicon carbide is SiC.

Diamond

Diamonds are the hardest material known to man and are almost pure carbon crystal. Both natural diamonds and manufactured (synthetic) diamonds are used for making sharpening stones and grinding wheels. Natural diamonds are used in both resin and metal-bonded diamond grinding wheels. Man-made or manufactured diamonds in shapes which provide a more friable abrasive for resin-bonded diamond wheels and sharpening stones are the choice for sharpening or grinding all carbide materials.

Cubic Boron Nitride

Cubic-structured boron nitrate is a man-made abrasive which approaches the diamond in hardness. It was developed as an outgrowth of synthetic diamond research by the General Electric Company (GE) and is marketed in the United States by GE under the tradename BORAZON™ CBN.

ABRASIVE ADHESIVES

The second part of any sharpening stone or grinding wheel (in addition to the abrasive itself is the adhesive or bonding agent used to hold the grains together in a usable form. At the present, there are five major bonding agents used in the industry and we will briefly discuss each.

Resinoid

Resinoid is a thermosetting resin. Resin-bonded grinding wheels are extremely durable and can be operated at high speeds—up to 16,000 s.f.p.m. Since this bonding agent is capable of withstanding severe and abusive grinding stresses, resinoid grinding wheels are currently the choice for high-speed rough grinding and cut off operations. They are also adaptable with fine grits to produce super-finishes on some precision grinding jobs. For certain applications, resinoid grinding wheels are reinforced for added strength.

Vitrified

Glassy-type, clay-type, and porcelain-eous-type bonds are used in the manufacture of vitrified bonding grinding wheels and sharpening stones. More than half of all grinding wheels made today are of the many types of vitrified bonds. Their rigidity provides fast, economical stock removal and makes them especially well suited to precision grinding up to about 12,000 s.f.p.m. as well as other general purpose grinding operations. Most sharpening stones are made using this bonding method.

Rubber

Both natural and synthetic rubbers are used as bonds in the manufacture of grinding wheels and sharpening stones. In softer types, the resiliency of this bond produces excellent polishing wheels. The harder types combine a degree of resiliency and water resistance for safe, cool-cutting cutoff wheels which are used when burr and burn of the metal must be held to a minimum. Other applications include grinding wheels and regulating wheels for centerless grinding.

Shellac

Shellac makes a low heat resistant bond resulting in very versatile grinding action with particular qualities of free-cutting action and good finish. Shellac generally has very limited use, mainly in the manufacture of roll grinding wheels.

Metal

Metal is used as a bonding agent only in the manufacture of diamond grinding wheels and sharpening stones. When metal-bonding is used it is strong, ductile, and, as you might expect, costly.

Sharpening stones—both man-made and natural—come in a variety of shapes, sizes, and configurations. The most basic of all are the common bench stones which are simply rectangular in shape. In addition, there are rounded, curved, tapered, and even grooved sharpening stone designs. The stone's intended purpose will usually dictate the design and composition. For example, when putting an edge on a knife, a flat bench stone is used; for sharpening a scythe (which has a curved blade and only one sharpened side), a special oval-sectioned stone is a far better choice. Throughout this book, when I talk about performing a sharpening operation with a stone, I will point out the recommended stone shape, size, and type for that particular task.

GRINDING WHEELS

Modern grinding wheels can remove large amounts of metal quickly and are therefore useful during some sharpening operations, especially when a tool edge has been chipped or otherwise damaged. Grinding wheels, however, work too quickly for standard sharpening tasks, such as putting a keen edge on a knife. This task is better accomplished on a common bench stone. In addition, if a grinding wheel is used incorrectly, you run the risk of overheating the tool and ruining its *temper*—the existing hardness of the metal. As a rule, if a piece of tool steel is heated up to a straw color—an easy task on a modern grinding wheel—the temper of the tool's steel will have been changed and as a result it will never be the same again. It is therefore possible to ruin a tool by trying to sharpen it on a grinding wheel (Fig. 1-3).

Grinding wheels do play an important part in reshaping tools prior to sharpening with a slower-working sharpening stone, providing that the proper grinding wheel is used for the work. At the present, almost all grinding wheels are man-made and there are hundreds of different grinding wheels available. For this reason we need to talk a bit about how grinding wheels are made, graded, and properly used.

The production and manufacture of modern grinding wheels is the result of many years of research and experience. All grinding wheels can rightly be considered precision cutting tools and are made according to specific industry-wide standards. As a result, grinding wheels are uniform throughout and can be relied upon to perform well throughout their range of capabilities.

The process of manufacturing modern grinding wheels begins by measuring precise amounts of abrasive grains of a uniform size.

Fig. 1-3. Excessive heat from grinding can ruin the temper in any tool.

As mentioned earlier, grains of abrasives are separated by passing the material through different sies of mesh screening. Electronically-controlled automatic weighing and mixing operations ensure that each grinding wheel is made up of exactly the right ingredients; uniformity throughout each wheel is guaranteed. Next, the abrasive grit is mixed with a bonding material—vitrified, resinoid, rubber, shellac or metal, as described earlier in this chapter. These two ingredients are mixed thoroughly and screened once again until complete uniformity is achieved. Then the abrasive/bonding agent mixture is pressed into a special mold which is in the shape of the desired grinding wheel. Within the molds, the mixture is hydraulically pressed to exact density or grain spacing. This grain spacing is commonly referred to as the "structure" of the grinding wheel and it is a very important step in the manufacturing process which we will cover later in this section.

The welding of the abrasive grit and bonding agent is achieved with heat in either kilns (which achieve high temperatures) or ovens (which offer much lower temperatures). Vitrified bonding grinding wheels are processed at temperatures approaching 2300 degrees F.

(kilns) while other bonding agents (such as resin, rubber or shellac) are heated in ovens which do not reach temperatures much above 400 degrees F.

Hardness and grade of every grinding wheel is monitored throughout the manufacturing process by various means including stroboscopic and sonic testing equipment and, in some cases, sophisticated machine penetration. If bushings, steel backs, or other mounting devices are required, these are secured after the grinding wheel has been fired. The next steps in the process include spin testing of all grinding wheels, further grading, and labeling.

Grinding wheels are labeled according to a marking system that is standard throughout the industry. It is possible, for example, to look at any American-made grinding wheel and determine its makeup, grade, bonding agent type, etc. Figure 1-4 shows the order of grinding wheel markings.

Earlier I mentioned grain structure in grinding wheels; let's examine a few points about this. In analyzing grinding wheel grain structure, it is important to understand that abrasive grain size (for a given grinding wheel)

remains constant. However, the *volume* of the abrasive grain will vary according to the structure of that particular wheel. For example, the volume of abrasive grain is greater in a dense structured wheel and the volume is less in open structured grinding wheels.

As a rule, the closer grain spacing is denoted by low structure numbers and such a wheel is regarded as being dense. Higher structure numbers indicate a more open grain spacing, or less density. It is important to keep in mind that the amount of space around each grain of abrasive grit is pre-determined and achieved by the bonding agent and the amount of hydraulic pressure applied to the abrasive/bonding agent mixture when it is poured into the mold. These voids around the abrasive grains allow the grains to escape as they become dull and useless at cutting or sharpening. The sharpness of the individual abrasive grains, the type of bonding agent used, and the intended application of the grinding wheel all are important factors in determining how the wheel is put together.

As with sharpening stones, grinding wheels are made from abrasive grains from four materials: aluminum oxide, silicon car-

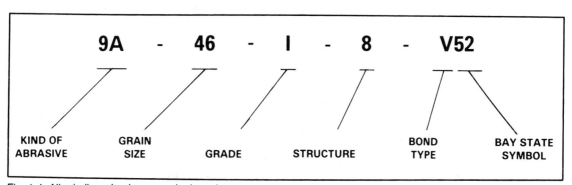

Fig. 1-4. All grinding wheels are marked as above.

bide, diamonds, and cubic boron nitride. Since there are differences in physical properties between these grinding wheel materials, it will be helpful to briefly mention the uses of each.

Aluminum oxide grinding wheels probably account for the largest part of grinding wheel makeup. In fact, if one wheel could be considered general purpose, aluminum oxide would be the choice. Generally speaking, aluminum oxide grinding wheels are used for grinding all steel alloys.

Silicon carbide grinding wheels are the second most popular type; because of their strength and quick cutting ability, they are used for grinding a wide range of hard and dense materials. The list includes all non-ferrous metals (aluminum, brass, copper, and bronze), cast and chilled iron, and most types of non-metallic materials (glass, stone, and ceramics).

Diamond grinding wheels are very hard and are used extensively in industry. They are ideal for grinding very hard materials such as carbide and cemented carbide, stainless steel, and high-carbon steel. Because diamond grinding wheels are expensive, it is probably a safe assumption that the average do-it-yourselver will not have one to work with.

Cubic boron nitride, as mentioned earlier, is a man-made abrasive materal that approaches the diamond in hardness. Since this material is not as expensive as diamond abrasive, it is used with greater frequency both in industry and at the consumer level. Cubic boron nitride grinding wheels are a good choice for grinding and sharpening very hard ferrous metals such as carbide, stainless steel, and high-carbon steel.

While there are hundreds of different shapes, sizes, and grinding wheel designs available, the home sharpener need really only concern himself with a few basic types. These include the *straight, straight cup*, and possibly *flared cup* design (Fig. 1-5). In fact, almost all home grinding can be done with the straight grinding wheel design. This is a good choice, as the straight design is readily available in a wide range of abrasives and grit sizes.

Bench Grinders

To take full advantage of modern grinding wheels, the do-it-yourselfer should have a good bench grinding machine. This electric tool can be used for a number of grinding tasks around the home workshop and it is therefore important that you exercise a certain amount of

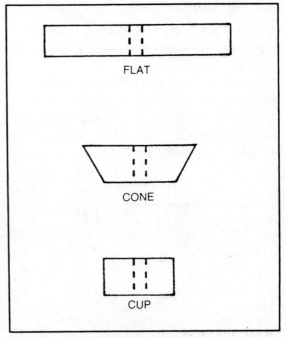

Fig. 1-5. Three basic designs of grinding wheels in use today—flat, cone, and cup.

care when buying one. At present, there are a number of good bench grinders available.

Modern bench grinders are rated according to how large a grinding wheel can be used on the machine. At present, these sizes range from the small 5-inch to the 8-inch heavy-duty models. In addition, all electric grinders also have a horsepower rating—about ¼ horse for the small hobbyist versions up to one horsepower for the heavy-duty bench grinders.

Probably the best all-around bench grinder for the do-it-yourselfer is one which has a horsepower ratio of from ½ to ¾ horse. Such a grinder will take grinding wheels up to 7×¾ inch and be powerful enough for all grinding tasks around the home. In addition,

there are a few other features that you will find useful on a bench grinder. These include a special "goose neck" light on the machine so you can clearly see as you work; adjustable tool rests in front of each wheel which enable you to perform precision grinding; adjustable and adequate clear plastic eye shields; and easily removable wheel covers (shielding the sides of the wheels). A bench grinder with these capabilities and attachments costs about $100—a small price for a machine that should last about ten years under normal conditions (Fig. 1-6).

Before using it, you must securely fasten your grinder to a workbench or special stand. This will not only enable you to use the grinder

Fig. 1-6. A good bench grinder is a useful tool around the home workshop (Garrett Wade Company).

safely, but it also helps you to take full advantage of its capabilities. When mounting your grinder on a workbench, position it close to the edge and far enough away from the walls so that you can lift long tools (such as a two-handed shovel) up to the machine. While a bench grinder is handy for many projects around the home, you will probably not use the unit frequently. For this reason, it is always best to locate your grinder so that it will not be in the way when you work on other projects in the home workshop. The end of the workbench is the usual and most convenient location of a bench grinder.

One very good alternative to mounting your grinder on the workbench is to make or buy a special stand for it. There are several good steel grinder stands available. Sears, for example, offers two different types. In addition, there are also three grinder stands that

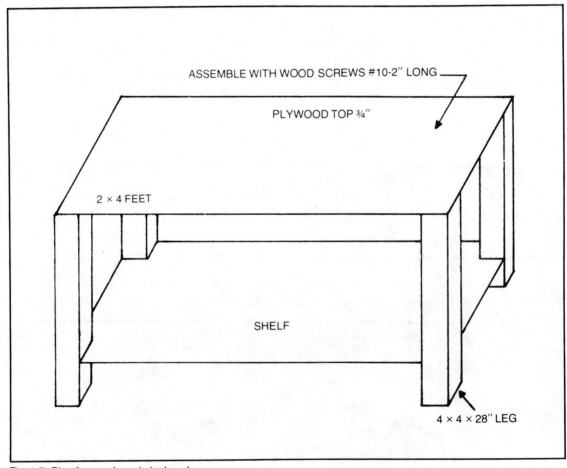

Fig. 1-7. Plan for wooden grinder bench.

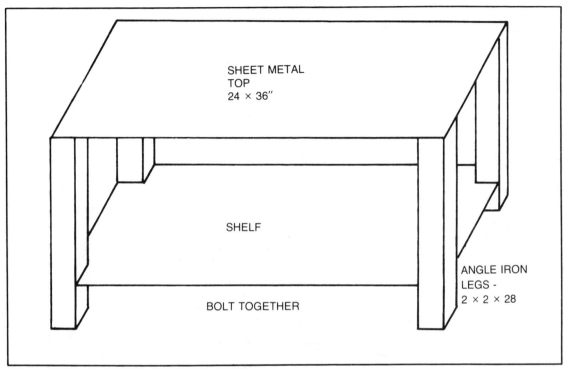

SHEET METAL
TOP
24 × 36″

SHELF

ANGLE IRON
LEGS -
2 × 2 × 28

BOLT TOGETHER

Fig. 1-8. Plan for metal grinder bench.

you can make in your home workshop. One stand is made from lumber and is portable (Fig. 1-7).

Another grinder workstand that you can make at home uses steel (1½ inch angle iron) and is constructed using bolts. Wheels can be added to make this grinder stand mobile—a very good idea, as the grinder can be moved around as needed (Fig. 1-8).

One last grinder stand that you can make in the home workshop requires a bit of welding. If you do not have welding equipment, you should be able to take the pieces to a local welder and have him do the work for a few dollars. This grinder stand (Fig. 1-9) is extremely sturdy but not portable.

Bench Grinder Safety

Grinding metal is a task that should never be approached casually, as the potential for injury always exists. There are a number of safety precautions that should always be taken whenever any grinding task is attempted. In addition, there are also a few things that you should do before attaching a new (or used) abrasive wheel to the grinder.

Abrasive wheels for bench grinding machines can be easily damaged if dropped, so it is important to handle them carefully. Before you mount a grinding wheel on a grinder, you should make certain that the wheel is in sound condition. This can be easily accomplished by tapping the wheel with a light wooden tool.

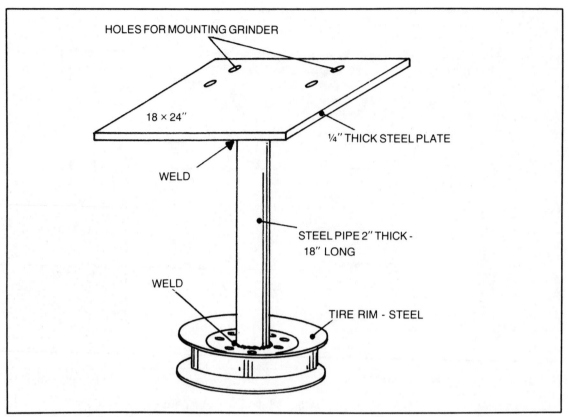

HOLES FOR MOUNTING GRINDER

18 × 24″

¼″ THICK STEEL PLATE

WELD

STEEL PIPE 2″ THICK - 18″ LONG

WELD

TIRE RIM - STEEL

Fig. 1-9. Plan for welded metal grinder table.

The wooden handle of a screwdriver works well for this. Suspend the wheel by slipping one finger through the center hole and then gently tap the side of the wheel in four places—north, south, east and west. Each tap should produce a clear ring. If tapping does not produce a ringing sound, you must look the wheel over *very* carefully to check for small cracks (Fig. 1-10).

When performing the ring test on a grinding wheel, it is important to know that different abrasive materials will produce rings with different tones. To give you some basis for comparison, know that vitrified and silicate wheels emit a clear metallic ring. Organic bonded wheels, on the other hand, usually give a less clear ring but it will be a ring nevertheless. A dull, non-metallic ring usually means that the wheel has a crack. In addition, oil or water-soaked wheels do not ring clearly. Grinding wheels which have been soaked or filled by the manufacturer to modify the cutting action of the wheel will sound dull but there will still be a ringing sound. Obviously, if a dead sound is produced by the tap test, you should inspect the grinding wheel for cracks. If

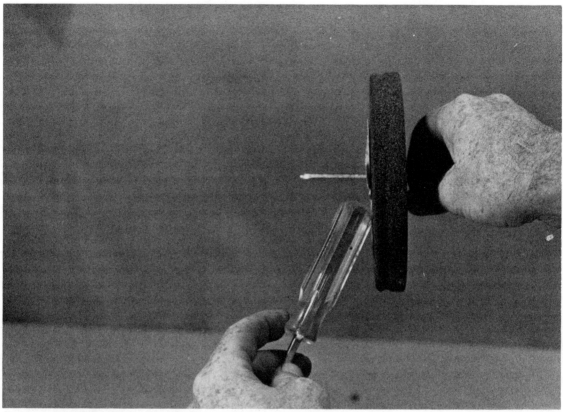

Fig. 1-10. A grinding wheel in good condition will have a distinctive ring.

any cracks are found, *do not* use the wheel. The chances are good of it coming apart when subjected to high rpm. If the wheel has never been used before, return it to the manufacturer for a replacement. If the grinding wheel is used or old, it is best to discard it. You could also use it as a bench stone, but never on a grinding machine.

When mounting a sound grinding wheel on a grinding machine, there are a few things that you must do to ensure that the task is done correctly. Since all straight abrasive wheels are mounted between two flanges, the actual fastening is fairly straightforward. It is important that both flanges be of the same diameter and should be perfectly true. In addition, the flanges should not be less than one-third the diameter of the abrasive wheel being attached.

Flange nuts should be tightened only enough to hold the wheel firmly in position and to prevent wheel slippage. Do not overtighten; this may distort the flanges or, worse yet, crack the abrasive wheel (Fig. 1-11).

After mounting an abrasive wheel on the grinding machine, the wheel guards must be reattached as well. When grinding wheels are

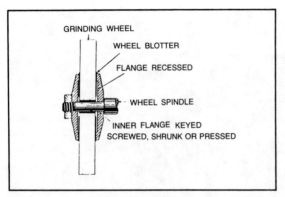

Fig. 1-11. The right way to install a grinding wheel on a machine.

not properly shielded with wheel guards, personal injury is possible if the wheel should accidently break during use.

Before you begin working on a grinding wheel, you should make sure you have plenty of work space. This will generally mean clearing the area around the machine. In addition, you should provide good lighting—both general shop lighting and specific lighting around the grinder.

When actually working on the bench grinder, you must always wear suitable eye protection. This may be a pair of plastic lens goggles or a face shield. It is a good safety practice to keep some type of eye protection on top of the grinding machine. This way you will be reminded to protect your eyes before turning on the machine. Do not rely solely on the plastic shields that are on most modern grinders. While these clear plastic shields offer some protection, they are inadequate as far as proper eye protection is concerned.

As you grind, work only on the front edge of the abrasive wheel. It is generally agreed that no grinding should be done on the side of

the wheel, as this will put undue strain on the wheel and increase the chance that it will break. Also, when grinding, it is important not to force work into the spinning wheel; this will put excess strain on the wheel as well.

Check the condition of your abrasive wheel often, especially when you are doing a lot of grinding. Occasionally the face of the wheel will clog with metal. When this happens, the face of the wheel will appear glazed and you will also notice that more pressure is required to grind. The best way to clean up a clogged abrasive grinding wheel is to use a special wheel dressing. This is simply a stick-like material that is pressed into the spinning wheel and which effectively rejuvenates it.

FILES

Another group of tools that is useful for some sharpening tasks are files. A file can remove large amounts of metal from a tool edge quickly. Unlike a grinding wheel, however, a file will not generally heat up metal during the process. For this reason, is a good choice for special metal removing or reshaping tasks. In some cases, a file is the tool used for the sharpening task—sharpening a chain saw chain for example. At other times, a file is used for developing an edge on a tool prior to final sharpening with a stone; an ax is a good example of this (Fig. 1-12).

To the untrained eye all files are the same, but to the experienced, there are a number of differences between them. Basically, files are grouped into two general categories—*single* and *double cut* files. For our purposes, this simply indicates the direction of the lines on the face of a file. On a single cut file, all the lines will run in one direction across

Fig. 1-12. Develop an edge bevel on an axe with a file, then finish off the sharpening with a stone.

the face of the file. On double cut files, these lines will all cross or be intersected by other lines with the overall effect of an "X" pattern (Fig. 1-13).

All files are made from very hard tool steel, a fact that makes the removal of metal with this tool possible. There are (as you might have guessed), several different types of steel alloys that are used in the production of files, but we will not get very far into metallurgy in these pages.

There are several file shapes or designs that the do-it-yourself home sharpener should be familiar with. These include the flat, round, triangular, and tapered files (Fig. 1-14). All of these basic file shapes are readily available wherever files are sold. Each of these files is designed for rather general use, as well as specific applications. For example, a round file

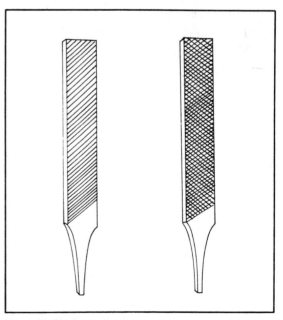

Fig. 1-13. Single cut file (left) and double cut file.

15

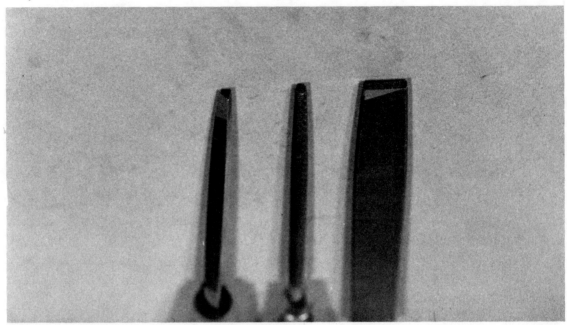

Fig. 1-14. The three basic file shapes—round, flat, and triangular.

can be used for sharpening the teeth in a saw chain, while a triangular file is used for touching up the edges of a handsaw's teeth. It is therefore important to choose the right file for the sharpening task at hand, providing of course that the task does indeed require a specially-shaped or designed file.

Besides choosing the right basic type of file for the task at hand, it is equally important to use the file properly. Most people who are not familiar with file use approach the task incorrectly. It is a fact that a file works best when pushed slowly into the work, and this is the best way to work a file—with slow, firm, deliberate strokes.

A file should never be used without a handle. Ironically, files are almost never sold with a handle. Instead, we find a selection of files and a selection of file handles. I suppose the reasoning behind this is that the file will wear out before the handle, so one handle can be used for a long line of files. In any event, you should not attempt to use a file without a handle. You can either purchase a few wooden file handles (and they will probably last a lifetime) or you can make your own handles in the home workshop. Personally, I prefer homemade file handles to commercial handles and they are easy to make.

The simplest of all file handles are made from wooden dowels. Three-quarter inch diameter dowels are ideal for small files; larger dowels—up to about 1½ inches in diameter— are great for the bigger files. The length of each handle should be approximately 4 inches for the average-size hand. If your hands are smaller or larger, adjust the length of your file handles to fit your hand.

After cutting a dowel to the desired length, drill a suitable hole in one end. For small files, a hole about ⅛th inch in diameter is suitable, but for larger files you will probably require a hole of at least ¼ inch. After a hole has been drilled in one end, round off the outer end with a wood rasp. Finish off the job with fine sandpaper and you can consider the handle ready for service.

Two added touches that will increase the life of your homemade file handles are to paint them and wrap wire around the hole end. The wire will help to prevent the handle from cracking in the event that the file is pushed too firmly into the handle. Bright acrylic paints

look good on file handles and will also make the handle easy to clean (Fig. 1-15).

There are a number of file guides and holders that are used for specific sharpening tasks—a chain saw sharpening guide is one example. File accessories such as these guide the file as it is used for sharpening and reduce the chances of using the file incorrectly. In Chapter 7 we will delve a bit deeper into file guides (Fig. 1-16).

A file will rust if it becomes wet and is then exposed to the atmosphere. One method used by some to prevent this is to spray files with a silicone spray such as WD-40. Such a lubricant will not affect how the file works but will effectively prevent rust.

As a file is used to remove metal from a

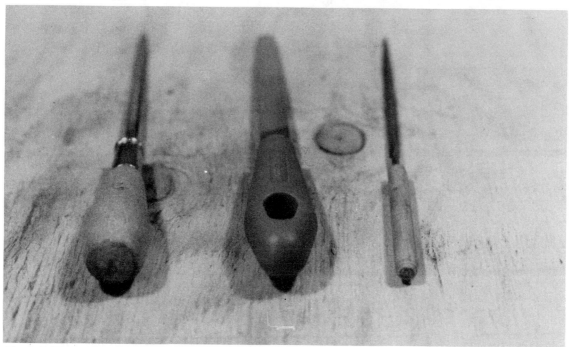

Fig. 1-15. File handles can be purchased or homemade.

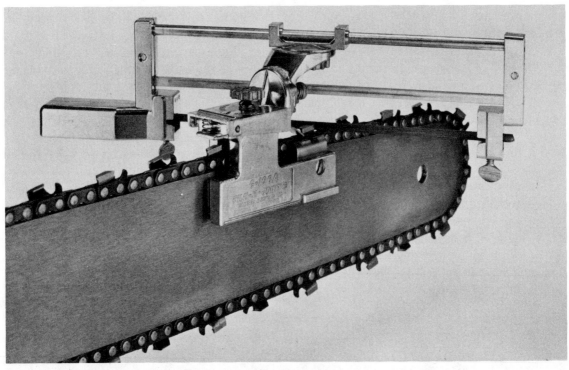

Fig. 1-16. The File-N-Joint is a handy attachment for sharpening a chain saw.

tool edge, the grooves in the face of the file may become clogged with tiny bits of metal. When this happens, the file is much less effective at cutting. If the file is not cleaned at this point it will not cut and will be useless. The only solution to this clogging problem is to clean the grooves in the file face. While there are several ways of doing this, the best involves the use of a special file card. This file cleaning tool is a good investment for the home craftsman for it will effectively extend the life of any file by keeping the grooves clean and sharp.

To use a file card, you simply brush the grooves on the file face with the steel bristles on one side of the card. The steel bristles will scrub out the grooves and make them almost as good as new. As you brush the grooves, you will see the tiny bits of metal coming free. After the file has been cleaned in this manner, the file card is turned over—the other side contains stiff fiber bristles—and the file is brushed again. The fiber bristles remove all of those tiny metal bits that the eye cannot see. Generally speaking, a file will be almost as good as new after it has been cleaned with a file card (Fig. 1-17).

LUBRICANTS

Whenever a bench sharpening stone is used for putting an edge on a tool, some type of lubricant should also be used. There are a

Fig. 1-17. Use a file card to clean the grooves in a file often.

number of lubricants that can be used during sharpening, and almost anyone who is familiar with stone sharpening has a favorite.

Probably the best stone lubricant to use for sharpening is one of the many oils that are offered by sharpening stone manufacturers. These are generally referred to as *honing oils*. When such an oil is not available, you can use almost any lightweight oil as a substitute. The choices include cooking oil, olive oil, medicinal mineral oil, Singer sewing machine oil, Three-in-One oil, and even kerosene. If nothing else is available, clear water can be used during sharpening.

Lubricants play a very important part in the sharpening process (when using a bench stone) so it is necessary to use some type of oil (Fig. 1-18). Oil on the surface of a sharpening stone helps to float off metal and abrasive dust that would otherwise become imbedded in the stone. If this were to happen, the stone would become clogged on the surface and useless at sharpening. One hard and fast rule about sharpening on a bench stone, then, is *always use some type of lubricating oil on the stone.*

A new sharpening stone should also be soaked in oil before use (unless, of course, the stone was oil-filled by the manufacturer). By soaking a bench stone in oil, you will make it easier to use and thus a more effective sharpening tool. Probably the best way to soak a stone is to place it in a small container and let it

Fig. 1-18. Oil is important when sharpening.

soak overnight in a lightweight mineral oil. After this initial soaking, wipe off the oil before use. During use, apply a few drops of oil to the surface of the stone. This will aid in carrying off abrasive dust and tiny bits of metal.

After using a bench stone for sharpening, wipe it off with a clean rag. Before you put it away, apply a few drops of clean oil to the stone. Store it in a wooden box with a cover, or in a Zip-Lock plastic bag. Covered storage is important, as dust and airborne material will clog the surface of a stone just as surely as abrasive dust and metal.

In time, all bench stones will require a thorough cleaning. Clean stones with a stiff fiber brush and kerosene until the surfaces have been restored, then resoak in mineral oil. If the surface of your bench stone should ever become glazed, clean with gasoline or lighter fluid and a stiff brush, or by rubbing the surface with a coarse abrasive paper. Re-oil the stone before use.

ABRASIVE PAPERS

Often during a sharpening task, it is helpful to use some type of abrasive paper for preparing the edge of the tool prior to sharpening with a bench stone. Abrasive paper is also handy for removing light rust on the surface of the tool and even for polishing the tool. Very often a tool's edge can be quickly touched up between serious sharpening with abrasive paper as well. Part of the beauty of abrasive paper is that it is relatively inexpensive to use.

For our purposes, abrasive papers that are useful for sharpening or touch-ups to a cutting edge are composed of a strong paper or cloth backing and a mineral grain face. The grains of abrasive are most commonly emery (which is a natural material) and silicon carbide (a man-made abrasive). Abrasive paper is available in a wide range of abrasive grit sizes. Coarse (about 80 grit) paper is a fast-cutting abrasive that is suitable for removing metal or rust from the surface of a tool. At the other end

of the spectrum we find abrasive paper with high numbers (such as 320) which actually polish more than cut. Papers in this group are generally referred to as *crocus cloth* and are very handy for touching up an edge on a tool.

The do-it-yourself sharpener should have a selection of abrasive papers in the home workshop. While abrasive papers are not really suitable for heavy-duty sharpening tasks, they are quite handy for touching up an edge on a tool and for removing surface rust and polishing.

You will find that using abrasive papers for light-duty sharpening is much easier to accomplish if you have some means of holding the paper flat and firmly as you work. One good way of holding the paper is to use a sanding block such as shown in Fig. 1-19.

Another type of abrasive paper holder can

Fig. 1-19. A sanding block can be used to sharpen a knife.

be easily made in the home workshop from a piece of scrap lumber. The simplest type of paper holder is made from a piece of 1×4 inch lumber approximately 8 inches long. A sheet of paper is fastened to this board with staples placed along both edges. This simple holder takes about two minutes to make and it will firmly hold abrasive paper while you touch up the edge on a tool. If you want to make the holder more useful, fasten coarse emery cloth on one side and extra fine grit paper on the other side. You can also start off with a longer 1×4 inch board and cut out the shape of a handle on one end with a sabre saw (Fig. 1-20).

OTHER SHARPENING AIDS

There are a number of sharpening aids, special tools, and hand-held sharpening machines that are currently available for the do-it-yourself home sharpener. Some of these aids (such as a barber's leather strop) have been around for centuries, while others, such as an electric saw chain sharpener, are relatively new. Let's look at a sampling of some of the more useful of these "gizmos."

The *barber's strop* mentioned earlier is a very handy (although vanishing) sharpening aid. A strop will not sharpen a dull knife or razor but it will touch up a fairly sharp knife edge and make it razor-sharp. You can make a similar strop from a smooth piece of leather. Fasten it to a board hair side up, and give it a coating of lightweight oil—SAE 20, for example. This simple homemade strop is very useful for putting a finishing touch to an already sharpened (on a bench stone) knife or tool. The

Fig. 1-20. Make a sanding block for sharpening by attaching sandpaper to a piece of scrap lumber.

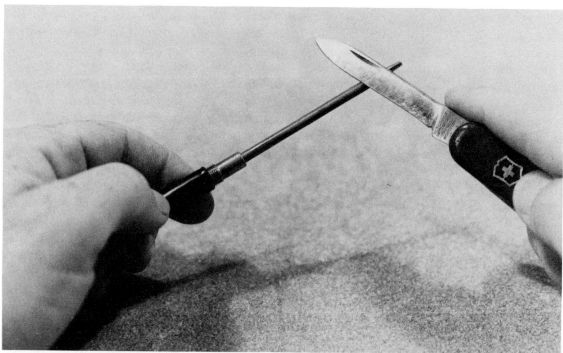
Fig. 1-21. A pocket steel is handy for on-the-spot sharpening tasks.

proper way to use a strop is to push the tool away and along the strop, with the edge *trailing*. Never push the tool with the cutting edge forward. This will dull the tool and probably cut the strop as well.

A *chef's steel* is very useful for touching up knives in the kitchen before a carving or cutting task. A chef's steel is simply a long tapered steel rod with tiny grooves (much like those on a single cut file) running the entire length. There are also grooveless and ceramic chef's steels available. It is important to keep in mind that a chef's steel does not have the ability to put an edge on a dull knife, but is used for touching up a knife that is almost sharp. A chef's steel can be used on a knife edge perhaps ten times before the knife must be reground

and sharpened properly. A steel works by turning up and breaking off a very fine feather edge on the blade, thus generating a new cutting edge. A chef's steel is a good addition to any kitchen. When buying a chef's steel, consider only those models that have a guard in front of the handle. Since a knife is stroked toward the handle, you run the risk of cutting yourself without such a guard (Fig. 1-21).

There are a number of useful electrically powered sharpening machines that have appeared in recent years. These include special grinders, like machines for sharpening saw chains, drill bits, and router bits. This may be a good time to talk a bit about these specialty sharpening devices.

A *twist drill bit sharpener* is a handy little

machine to have around the home workshop, especially if you do a lot of drilling. Generally speaking, there are two types of twist drill bit sharpeners available; those which have an internal motor, and those which require the use of an electric drill for power. Each has advantages and disadvantages. The self-contained twist drill bit sharpener offers convenience. Simply turn a switch and it is ready to sharpen most size twist drill bits. On the negative side, the self-contained drill bit sharpener costs around thirty dollars. The twist drill bit sharpener that requires the use of your electric drill for operation is inexpensive—about half the price of the self contained unit. This unit is also small enough to store easily in a standard drill case. About the only weak point about this unit is that it requires you to hook up your electric drill before you can use it. While this task is not difficult, it does consume a bit of time and prevents you from using your drill for anything else at the time. In any event, either of these twist drill bit sharpeners works well at restoring the tip to most standard size drill bits and is a worthwhile investment for the do-it-yourselfer.

A *belt sander* can also be used for some types of sharpening operations around the home. Generally speaking, this electric sanding tool—of which there are two suitable types—is most effective when used to put a working edge on garden tools as well as other tools that do not require a razor-sharp cutting edge (scissors, for example). The two best types of belt sanders for this type of sharpening are a common hand-held belt sander, and a stationary or bench-mounted type which uses an abrasive belt of about one inch in width. As a rule, the finer grit or grades of abrasive belts work best for most types of sharpening tasks.

If you do a lot of woodworking with a router, you should consider buying a special *router bit sharpening attachment.* This device, which clamps onto your router, securely holds any router bit while a special sharpening wheel spins. This sharpening bit is chucked into the router. The holding mechanism is fully adjustable so you can sharpen any size router bit. In addition, the sharpening wheel is a very hard man-made material that can sharpen both hard steel and carbide tipped router bits. A router bit sharpening device—which is most commonly sold in kit form—is a very worthwhile investment for the home craftsman who does a lot of woodworking with a hand-held router.

It is certainly no secret that thousands of Americans are now using wood heat as a supplement to or in place of conventional heating. Directly related to this trend is a growing body of do-it-yourselfers who own and maintain chain saws. As users become more experienced with chain saw operation, they realize that a sharp chain saw works best. As a result, many now touch up the cutters on saw chains. In the past, this touching up was done by hand with a file. In the past few years, those of us who use chain saws have seen the introduction of a number of devices which are designed not only to touch up the cutters on a saw chain but to sharpen them as well, thereby eliminating the need for a professional sharpening service. A quick look at the current offering reveals a wide selection of file guides, hand-held sharpeners (both electrically and battery operated), and sharpening devices which are used with a hand-held electric drill. Some of these saw chain sharpeners are truly not worth the metal they are made from, but many are very worthwhile and will, when used properly, effectively sharpen a saw chain. Two of these sharpening devices that are good are the Chainsaver (by the Dremel Company) and Pro Sharp (from the Pro Sharp Corporation).

The Dremel Chainsaver (Fig. 1-22) is a hand-held, electrically-powered saw chain sharpener that is simple to use and which will help you to touch up and sharpen your saw chain. While we will not explain how this sharpening device works here (detailed information can be found in Chapter 7). I would like to mention at this point that this tool is a worthwhile investment. In fact, the Dremel Chainsaver will virtually eliminate the need to take your saw chains to a professional grinder for sharpening. Each sharpening kit comes with a selection of man-made sharpening stones that will enable you to sharpen any saw chain you may come in contact with. A unique guidance system makes sharpening individual chain cutter teeth practically foolproof. The Chainsaver is very fast at sharpening—each tooth takes only a few seconds. Complete operating and sharpening instructions some with each unit so you can begin sharpening almost as soon as you take the unit out of its box. This is truly a worthwhile saw chain sharpening device and one that I highly recommend for anyone who has need for a sharp chainsaw.

The Pro Sharp (Fig. 1-23) is another saw chain sharpening device that is handy for put-

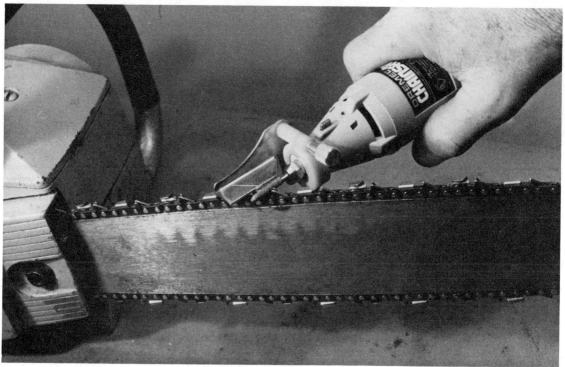

Fig. 1-22. The Dremel electric chain saw sharpener is very handy.

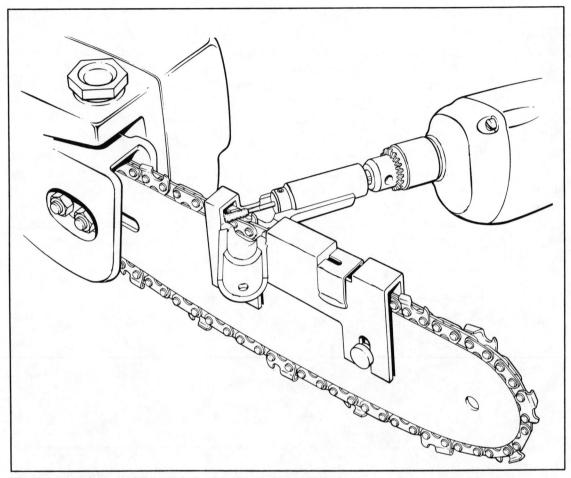

Fig. 1-23. The Pro Sharp chain saw sharpener uses your electric drill to work.

ting a keen edge on your saw. The Pro Sharpener is actually a two-part affair—the guidance system, and the sharpener itself. To use, you simply attach the guidance unit to the bar of your chain saw. Then you chuck the sharpening tool into your ¼ inch electric drill, which is the power behind the Pro Sharp. Next, the sharpening tool is positioned in the guidance unit and the electric drill is turned on. The guidance unit is made in such a way as to perfectly align

the sharpening tool with each saw chain tooth, so sharpening takes only a few seconds to accomplish. When used correctly, the Pro Sharp will enable you to sharpen any saw chain in a matter of minutes, and the sharpening will be on a level with a professional sharpening (Fig. 1-23).

There are a number of other sharpening devices and gizmos currently available and it seems that new additions to this field are introduced often. Evaluation of these sharpening devices would easily take up all of the pages in this book. In the final analysis, you must be the judge of the usefulness of any "revolutionary" sharpening tool. Generally speaking, if the tool is designed for a *specific* sharpening task, it is probably useful providing you require this specialty sharpening often. More often than not, however, you can achieve about the same results with conventional sharpening tools such as grinding wheels, files, and bench stones. As you will see in the following chapters, most sharpening tasks are accomplished with simple sharpening tools. Where a specialized sharpening tool or aid is called for, I will make mention of the fact.

Chapter 2

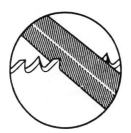

Knives

A dull knife is one of the most useless and frustrating tools in the kitchen, field, or workshop. Since you cannot control the cutting action of a dull knife, you are just as likely to cut yourself as what you are working on, and the cut you will receive will actually be worse than a cut from a sharp knife. The only type of knife you should *ever* use is a sharp one. By the end of this chapter, you will know how to go about putting a keen edge on any knife.

Knife sharpening is not difficult but many people make it so for some unknown reason. If a blade has not been damaged and you are not trying to change the basic design or bevel, then it should only be a matter of minutes before you can put a decent working edge on almost any knife.

Before we can intelligently talk about how to go about sharpening a knife blade, we need first to take a brief look at the various types of cutting edges that are in common use. Any knife you might pick up will have one of four possible edges: cannel, hollow, concave, or V-grind. Let's look at each of these and see what particular purpose each has been developed for.

CUTTING EDGES

The *cannel* edge or grind on a knife edge produces a strong cutting tool that can be used for heavy-duty cutting. A good example of an effective use of this edge design is a meat cleaver. Since this tool requires a blade with plenty of metal behind the edge for chopping through bones in a manner similar to an ax, the cannel edge is the best choice (Fig. 2-1).

The *hollow* or *hollow ground* cutting edge is a popular grind for general purpose cutting

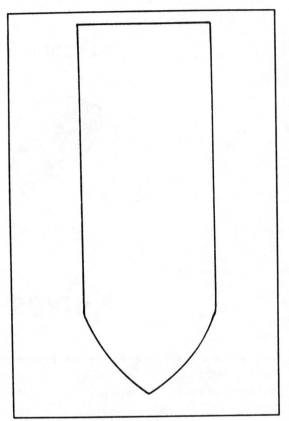

Fig. 2-1. Cannel knife edge design.

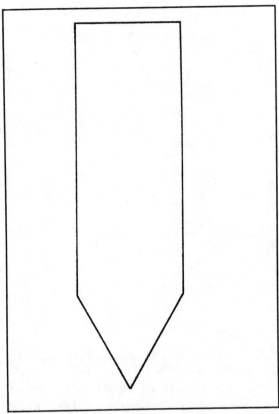

Fig. 2-2. Hollow ground knife edge design.

and is probably the most common edge on pocket and sheath knives. Because of the wide bevel, this edge is easy to work with on most materials (Fig. 2-2).

The *concave* edge design, some people feel, is even better for carving than the hollow ground blade, and is therefore used on many fine carving tools. Very thin slices of material are possible with this edge, so it is also an effective design in the kitchen as well as the workshop (Fig. 2-3).

The *V-grind* is a sturdy cutting edge and is very common on butcher knives and kitchen knives. While it does not stand up to continued use, it can be sharpened quickly on a butcher's steel (Fig. 2-4).

These four blade bevels are considered the standards in the industry, but a knife blade may in fact be a combination of any two. For example, the typical pocketknife blade is basically a V-grind design but the cutting edge will, in most cases, be hollow ground. This approach to edge sharpening leaves enough metal behind the cutting edge to give strength and durability to the blade (Fig. 2-5).

There are a number of different approach-

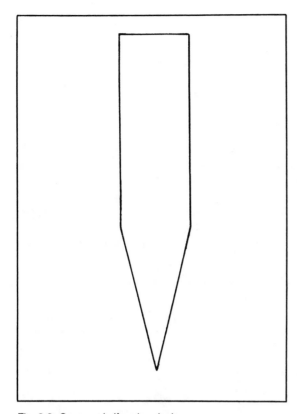

Fig. 2-3. Concave knife edge design.

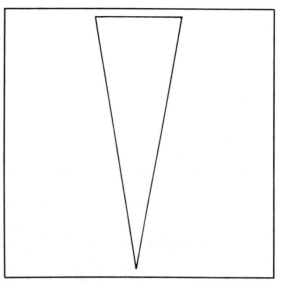

Fig. 2-4. V-Grind knife edge design.

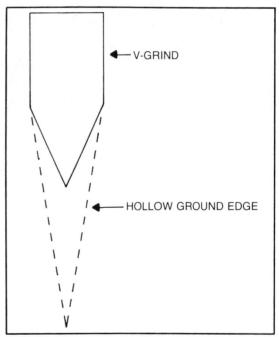

Fig. 2-5. Double design knife edge, common on pocket-knives.

es to sharpening a knife blade, and this is where most people become confused. After all, there are hundreds of different machines, gadgets, and sharpening aids on the market, in addition to the basic tools for sharpening—files, steels, stones (of which there are many types), belt sanders, and bench grinders. In an effort to take as much of the confusion as possible out of sharpening a knife, we will for the most part discuss knife sharpening with the basic sharpening equipment. This will give you a solid background and understanding of what is really involved. At the end of this chapter we will have a look at some of the sharpening aids and explain how they are used.

USING A BENCH GRINDER

As a rule, the only time a bench grinder should be used to sharpen a knife is when the blade has been damaged—either nicked or broken at the tip (Fig. 2-6). The heat generation of the average bench grinder will take the temper out of a knife blade in seconds, so you must always be careful not to let the blade get too hot during the grinding. Keep a container of water close by while working, and dip the blade often to cool. You should also use a very light touch. In other words, don't force the grinding.

You should know that there are some bench grinders that do not develop much heat as a result of being cooled by water during the sharpening process. If you do much knife sharpening, a cool-running bench grinder might be a good investment for you (Fig. 2-7).

Begin by adjusting the tool rest so that when the knife blade is placed here, the wheel will grind off at a perfect 90 degree angle. Grind the edge of the knife in this manner, keeping the blade moving constantly so that flat spots will not develop. Grind the blade until the nicks disappear. If the damage is slight, this may take only one or two passes on the blade. If the damage is significant, you must make several passes to remove the damaged area. In this case, stop often and dip the blade into the container of water. If the point of the knife blade has been damaged, the same technique is used to reestablish the curve and point (Fig. 2-8).

After the damaged area has been ground away, you must next readjust the tool rest to

Fig. 2-6. A chipped or nicked knife edge will need grinding or filing to remove the damaged area.

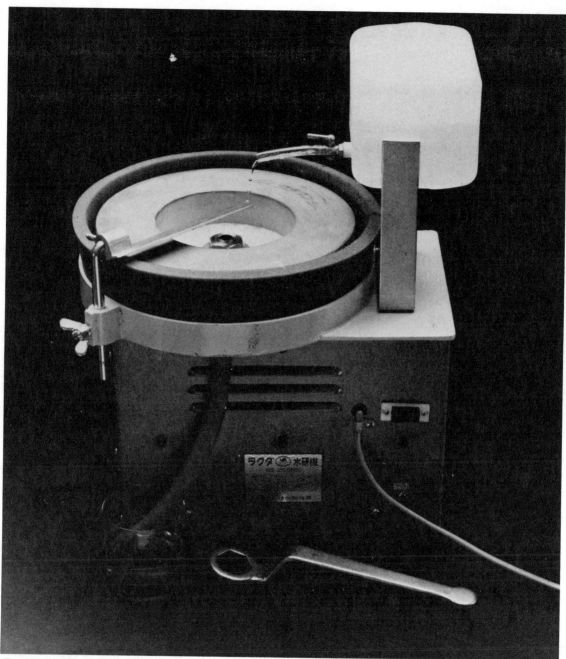

Fig. 2-7. A water-cooled grinding wheel will not heat up steel (Garrett Wade Company).

Fig. 2-8. The damaged area is ground off the knife blade.

the proper bevel angle. Some do-it-yourselfers like to grind the bevel freehand and this is possible only if you have a good eye and work very carefully. In any event, grind the bevel first on one side of the blade, then flip it over and grind the same bevel on the other side. When grinding, look for a fine wire edge, which will develop when the bevel has been achieved. After both sides have been ground properly, the next step is to finish off the sharpening on a bench stone.

There is another technique that can be used to repair a damaged knife blade that poses almost no danger to the temper of the steel; it involves the use of a flat file. Begin by clamping the knife into a bench vise so that the blade is held securely and at a comfortable working height. Next take the file and, holding its flat side perpendicular to the damaged knife edge, stroke the blade to remove the damage. Begin filing well behind the nick, and with a long stroke, pass over the area and beyond (Fig. 2-9). The strokes of the file should be long, smooth, and even. The reason for beginning and ending the filing before and after the damaged area is so that you will be able to maintain the original contour of the blade, while at the same time repairing the damage. As you file, you will notice that the edge of the blade will become flat and much wider than when you started—how wide, of course, depends on the extent of the damage. After the damage has been repaired, you must then bevel the edge. This can be done with a file or stone. If the area is very thick (over 0.005 inch), you will have a lot of metal to bevel and will probably be better off using the file for most of the work. If the nick was not too deep, you did not have to remove too much metal; therefore the beveling and sharpening can be accomplished on a stone.

USING A BENCH STONE

I think it is safe to say that the most common tool for sharpening a knife is a stone. It is also true that most do-it-yourselfers do not use a sharpening stone correctly. By the end of this section you will have a better understanding of the process.

Probably the handiest stone to have around the workshop is a combination stone. One side will be coarse (around 100 grit size) and the other side will be fine (around 600 grit size). Stones of this variety come in several sizes and range in price from around $8 for a pocket version to over $25 for a large bench stone. Most combination stones are man-made, so you can be fairly certain as to uniformity.

A good combination stone will enable you to put a keen edge on almost any knife you come across, so it is a good investment. Since it can also be used for sharpening a number of other tools, such as a wood chisel, a combination bench stone is handy around the workshop.

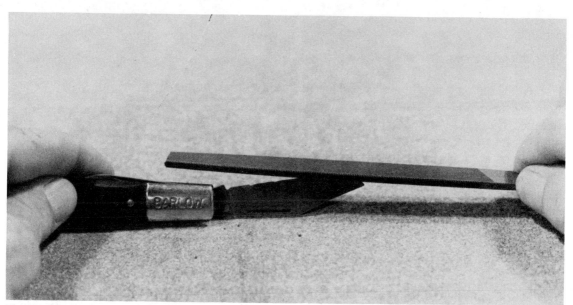

Fig. 2-9. Damaged area on knife blade being removed with a flat file.

Fig. 2-10. The best way to sharpen a knife is on a good stone.

To sharpen a knife, begin by placing the stone—coarse side up—on the edge of a table or bench. Next, add a few drops of honing oil to the surface. Use a special oil designed for the purpose or any lightweight oil or kerosene. Then, holding the knife behind the hilt, begin passing the blade over the stone. The cutting edge of the blade can *either* be leading or trailing—there are many theories here—but most importantly, the blade should be held at the desired edge bevel. Probably the best bevel angle for a general purpose cutting edge is around 15 degrees off the stone (Fig. 2-10).

For all but the dullest or recently ground knives, no more than 20 strokes per side should be required to develop a 15 degree bevel. The procedure is to make one pass, then turn the blade over and go back over the stone to complete one pass. While it is relatively easy to hold the blade at a 15 degree angle for the straight part of the cutting edge, as you near the tip of the knife, you must lift up slightly while at the same time developing the bevel around the point. Sometimes, especially with long knives, it is best to sharpen the blade in stages—first the straight part of the blade, then the curved tip.

If you sharpen only on the coarse side of

Fig. 2-11. Clean up a worn stone with a sanding block.

the combination stone, you should develop a very good cutting edge that will be suitable for a variety of cutting tasks. But you may want the knife sharper for a specific task such as cleaning game or fish, or whittling. If this is the case, after you have achieved a fairly sharp cutting edge on the coarse side of the stone, flip it over, apply a few drops of oil, and begin re-sharpening in the same manner. After about 20 passes you should have an almost razor-sharp edge on the knife.

Problems in sharpening a knife, can be due to several factors. First, you may be holding the knife at the wrong angle. Remember that an angle of about 15 degrees will give a good general purpose cutting edge, but you must hold the blade angle *consistently* throughout the sharpening stroke. This is a technique that is developed over time and only with con-

centration. Once you develop a knack for holding a consistent angle, 99 percent of your sharpening problems will be solved.

Another possible cause of problems when sharpening is a stone that is not flat. With time, all stones will develop a slight indented curve. This is a result of the nature of the work sharpening stones are called upon to do, it is quite normal. Nevertheless, a "bellied" stone is difficult to sharpen on so you should make the surface flat by sanding before using the stone for a sharpening task.

To check the flatness of the surface of a bench stone—and *always* suspect old stones are being bellied—lay it flat on a piece of 80 grit sandpaper and rub for a few moments in a circular motion. Lift the stone off the abrasive paper and look at the surface. If tiny scratch marks are evenly dispersed across the surface, the stone is flat. But (as is often the case) if only the ends of the stone show any signs of scratches, then the center of the stone is worn more. To correct this problem and restore a flat surface to your stone, simply run the stone over the abrasive paper in a circular motion with the curved side down (Fig. 2-11). This action will also clean the surface pores of the stone which often become clogged with oil and tiny particles of steel from previous sharpenings. Remember to oil the stone heavily after sanding.

USING A BUTCHER'S STEEL

One of the handiest sharpening aids to have in the kitchen is a butcher's steel sharpening rod. There are several types on the mar-

ket. Some are made from a ribbed steel rod, some are fairly smooth, and still others are made from ceramic or man-made stone. In any case, they all work in the same manner and are very useful for restoring the edge to a carving knife or any other knife in the kitchen. If you watch a professional butcher at work, you will probably notice that he gives a few swipes of his knife to a steel before cutting up a meat order. You will want to do the same if you have a cutting task at hand that requires a razor-sharp edge.

To use a butcher's steel, begin by holding it in your left hand with the knife to be sharpened in your right (if you are right-handed), cutting edge downward. Next, begin making a pass down along the steel by starting at the tip

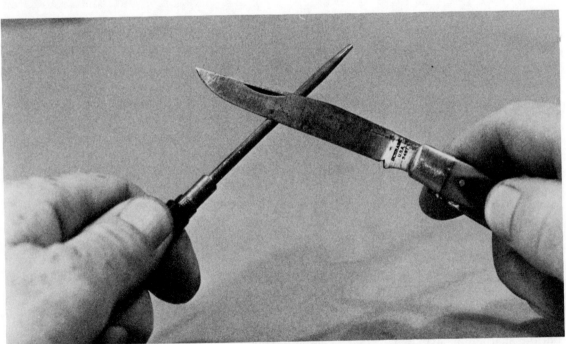

Fig. 2-12. A sharpening steel is handy for putting a razor edge on a knife blade.

of the steel with the back edge of the knife. As you swipe down the handle, pull the knife towards you so that the entire edge of the blade passes over the steel along the way. As you near the end of the stroke, bend your wrist so that the area along the front of the knife blade passes over the steel as well. Give one stroke to one side of the blade, then make a pass with the other side of the blade touching the steel. You must hold the knife so that it is at an approximate angle of 15 degrees throughout the entire stroke. In most cases, five or six passes per side should develop a razor-like edge on the blade (Fig. 2-12).

If you are not able to develop a sharp edge on a knife with a butcher's steel, you may be holding the blade at the wrong angle. Remember that an angle of about 15 degrees will give the best edge. Another possibility for failure of a butcher's steel is clogged grooves. As a knife is sharpened, microscopic pieces of steel are worn away and held in the grooves. In addition, a steel will become magnetized in time—unless it came magnetized, as most do—and this action will also hold ground metal on the surface. To clean up a used butcher's steel, wipe it with a cloth which has been dampened in vegetable oil. You will be amazed at how much material will come off with just a few wipes. Then wipe the steel again with a dry cloth to remove the oil. The sharpening ability of any butcher's steel will be greatly enhanced with this treatment.

KNIFE SHARPENING AIDS

There are probably more gadgets, gizmos, and other so-called "knife sharpeners" than types of natural sharpening stones. While researching this book I discovered quite a few

and must admit that some of these devices will help sharpen a knife, even if the user has never been able to sharpen a knife in the past. In just about every case, however, the device sharpens largely as a result of holding the knife blade at a consistent angle, or forces the user to hold a knife at a predetermined angle, most commonly 15 degrees. Since this is probably the most difficult part of sharpening for the beginner, such a sharpening aid should work for anyone. But if you can hold this angle freehand, you can usually do a better sharpening job with just a combination stone (Fig. 2-13).

A popular addition to most electric can openers is a knife sharpener, usually on the

Fig. 2-13. For a keen edge, draw the knife across the stone.

back of the unit. These tiny sharpeners are handy for general sharpening. A sharpener of this type, however, will not sharpen a knife forever. In time, the blade will require a proper sharpening on a bench stone.

Another knife sharpening system consists of two (usually triangular) ceramic or man-made stone rods which are held in a V shape on some type of wooden or plastic base. These sharpeners work nicely and are popular for that reason. The theory behind these sharpeners is that the 15 degree angle is maintained as you push a knife blade downwards along the shaft. Such a sharpening device will put an almost razor-sharp edge on any knife, so they are a worthwhile investment for the kitchen (Fig. 2-14).

One other sharpening aid that I find worthwhile is the Loray Sharpener (available from many mail-order houses or from Loray Sharpeners, 16740 Indian Hollow Road, Grafton, Ohio 44044). The Loray Sharpener is actually a set of sharpening stones—100, 320, and 600 grit—honing oil, knife blade holder, stone holder, and guide. It is just the ticket for sharpening many of the harder steel knives that seem to be popular (Fig. 2-15).

The Loray Sharpener, when used with

Fig. 2-14. A popular sharpening device.

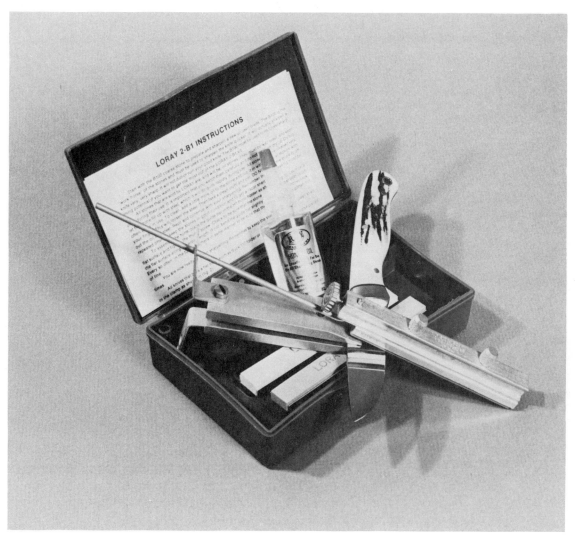

Fig. 2-15. The Loray Sharpening System comes with all necessary parts.

optional bench mount, holds a knife blade steadily, leaving your hands free while one of the three stones is passed over the cutting edge. The angle of the stone is ensured by the special holder it rests in, a rod affair that is guided through bevel angle holes at the back of the blade holder. First one side of the blade is given a pass, then the stone holder is switched to the other side and it receives a pass of the stone. This continues, side for side, until the knife is sharp. This usually takes about four passes per side. The system is so easy to use

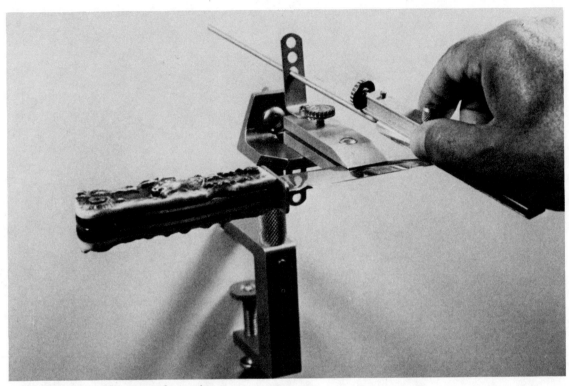

Fig. 2-16. The Loray Sharpening System in use.

that it takes about one minute to sharpen even the longest, dullest knife in the house. It's certainly a worthwhile investment for the do-it-yourselfer (Fig. 2-16).

Chapter 3

Hand Woodworking Tools

The typical home shop will contain a variety of hand tools used for home maintenance, woodworking projects, and just about any other little task that comes along. Woodworking tools not only work better but also last longer if they are used only with a keen edge. Unfortunately, not all hand woodworking tools have the same type of cutting edge so they obviously cannot all be sharpened in the same manner. In an effort to touch all bases, this chapter categorizes all tools into one of three rather broad groups: tools that *cut*, tools that *shape*, and tools that *bore or make holes*. What makes each group different is the type of cutting edge (or edges) that are present on a representative tool.

In the group of tools that cut, we obviously would find saws of several types, knives, and shears. These tools might also be used for cutting tasks around the home and workshop.

The other two groups contain tools that have a cutting edge of a special type as you will see. It is important to remember that just about any tool will have some type of cutting edge; in all cases, this edge will work most efficiently when it is sharp. It is not possible to accomplish a cutting, shaping, or boring task with a dull tool.

HANDSAWS

Undoubtedly, the most common cutting tool in the home workshop is the *handsaw*. Here we will also find the *hacksaw, keyhole saw,* and *finish saw* in addition to the more common *rip* and *crosscut saws*. To be sure, there is an apparent trend to grab an electrically-powered saw for a cutting task rather than a muscle-powered tool, but on those occasions where you have the time, you will find

Fig. 3-1. If you have the time, working with a handsaw is enjoyable.

hand sawing a rewarding experience. It should also be noted that fine-edged and straight cuts are the rule when a sharp handsaw is used for a cutting task. If time permits, cutting with a handsaw is one of those wood working joys that some people look forward to—this author included (Fig. 3-1).

Another reason for using a hand-powered saw for a cutting task might be that electrical power may not be readily available, although with the availability of portable electrical generating equipment you can usually find a source of power.

One other reason for choosing a handsaw might be the pure and simple satisfaction that

is attached to work of this nature. Without the noise and bulk of power tools, you are able to feel closer to the work and therefore are in a better position to be one with the work. The end result, as anyone who knows will testify, is a project you can be proud of.

This may be a good time to review some of the basics of handsaw design. It is certainly no secret that part of the reason many of us do not use a handsaw is largely because we are unfamiliar with its capabilities. We can then all benefit from a brief discussion of what makes a good handsaw.

To begin with, any saw is only as good as the material and workmanship that goes into

Fig. 3-2. A quality handsaw will be made from good steel and will usually say so on the blade.

making it. A quality handsaw will be made of special steel, for this is one of the distinguishing marks of any select tool (Fig. 3-2). Steel used in sawmaking must be durable—in this case, hard and tough—in order to hold a cutting edge. In addition, it must also be sturdy enough to withstand buckling. In better saw steel, this is accomplished through metallurgically tempering special steel to an exact degree. The end result is an extremely tough saw that will hold an edge through long periods of use while at the same time having the right amount of resilience to withstand buckling yet permit proper filing and setting of the individual teeth.

It is probably safe to say that most handsaws are taper ground. This tapers the entire blade from teeth to back, so that the blade resembles an inverted wedge. The *kerf*—sometimes called the *cut*—made by the teeth is wide enough to permit the body of the saw to fit easily, reducing the natural tendency of the saw to bind or buckle.

One last thing to consider when answering the question "what makes a good handsaw" is the shape and positioning of the handle, for this will have an effect on how well the saw performs. The handle should be designed to direct the saw's energy straight to the cutting teeth and not against the back of the saw. A well-positioned handle will not strain the wrist

Fig. 3-3. The handle on a good saw will fit the hand well.

and will, in fact, make every ounce of your sawing energy count (Fig. 3-3).

When shopping for a new handsaw (or possibly a quality used tool), there are several points that you should check with the saw in hand:

☐ Tension—To check the tension of a saw, it should be flexed slightly and a straight edge placed across the blade. The gap between the straight edge and saw blade should form a perfect arch. A lopsided bow indicates a poorly balanced saw (Fig. 3-4).

☐ Teeth—Hold the saw at arm's length.

Bend the blade slightly to bring the points of the teeth into view along the breast of the blade. Points along the blade edge should all be the same length. Look along the flat sides of

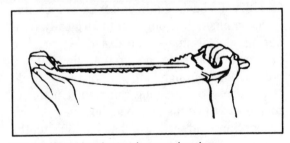

Fig. 3-4. Checking the tension on a handsaw.

the blade and examine it for a uniform set. Poor setting of the teeth will cause the saw to cut inaccurately.

☐ Finish—A quality handsaw should look and feel good. There should be no ridges, nicks, or rough spots along the blade. It is important to keep in mind that a smooth, highly-polished finish will resist rust in addition to helping to cut down on friction when cutting. Even the handle on a quality handsaw will be finished well and pleasing to both the hand and eye.

As with most things in life, there is a right and a wrong way to use a handsaw. For the benefit of those of you who may never have learned, let's quickly review how to properly use a handsaw. You will find handsawing much easier when the saw is held correctly. When using a crosscut saw, for example, the saw, wrist, and forearm should form a straight line at an angle of 45 degrees to the work. With a ripsaw, a steeper angle of about 60 degrees is required for most efficient cutting. In either case, it is important always to keep your eye on the work and always to cut to the waste side of the work (Fig. 3-5).

To start a cut, begin with a few short strokes, steadying the saw with the thumb of the freehand. Be extremely careful at this point, for there is a tendency for the blade to hop and cut your fingers. After a groove has been cut, continue sawing with long, steady strokes. They are easier on you and the saw. A short, jerky motion, on the other hand, wastes energy and causes uneven tooth wear. Long, smooth strokes gives faster cutting and much better control. Use just enough pressure to keep the saw from chattering. By forcing the feed, you may upset the saw's balance. This is

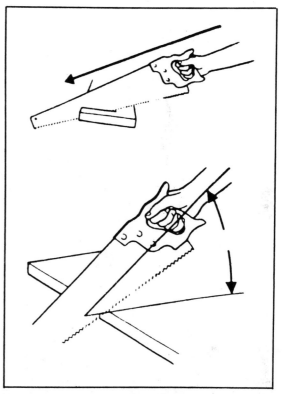

Fig. 3-5. Proper angles for holding a handsaw.

particularly true when cutting through a knot. Since the knot is much harder than the rest of the wood, it will call for slower—*not* faster—cutting speed.

Always support the waste end with your free hand until the cut is completely through (Fig. 3-6). Letting waste ends break off by themselves sometimes causes work to split. Also guard against twisting the saw to knock off waste ends. This can not only ruin the tooth setting but possibly also break a tooth or two.

Properly cared for and treated, a good handsaw will last for many years. To ensure a long and useful life, there are a number of things that should be done to your handsaw in

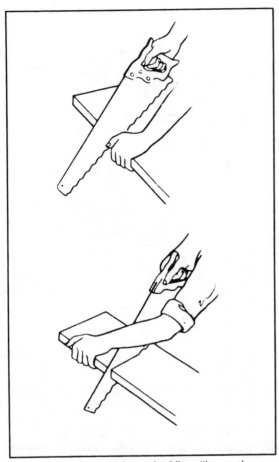

Fig. 3-6. You must hold the work while cutting as shown.

If you should ever discover rust on your handsaw, you should try to remove it as quickly as possible. If the rust is just a light coating on the surface, often a quick wipe with an oily rag will remove it. If, however, the rust has established a firm foothold, you must resort to more aggressive tactics. For removing medium to heavy rust you must use an abrasive paper—emery cloth usually works well—and water. The usual technique is to wet the saw and place it rusty side up on a piece of dimensional lumber such as a suitably long piece of 2×8. Next, emery cloth is used in conjunction with the water to rub the rust away. As you can well imagine, your work will be determined by the amount and depth of the rust you are removing. Circular motions work best with the area kept wet by frequent applications of water. You may also find the addition of some valve grinding compound helpful. This abrasive paste is available at any automobile parts shop. If nothing else, removing the rust from a favorite saw will be a lesson in keeping all handsaws—and other metal tools—lightly oiled in the future.

When not in use, a handsaw should be hung out of harm's way in the workshop. If you find it necessary to carry your handsaw around with other tools, you should cover the blade with some type of protective wrapping, such as the slip-case it was sold in, to prevent damage to the surface and teeth. Some traveling woodworkers like to keep all handsaws in a special handsaw carrying box. While this special saw box is another thing to carry around, it will also be the most long-lived storage you could ask for.

No matter how much tender loving care you give to your favorite handsaw, the fact remains that if you use it often, it will eventu-

addition to keeping it sharp, as you will see a bit later on. The first thing you should do for your quality handsaw is to keep a light coat of oil on the metal surfaces. Either a light spray with a good silicone such as WD-40, or a light coating of oil applied with a rag is probably the best insurance against rust. After using the saw, you should once again give it a light coating of silicone spray or oil. Get into the habit of doing this each and every time you use the saw and it will last a lifetime.

ally lose its fine cutting edge and you will learn that it requires more effort on your part to use. When this stage is reached there are only two real choices as to the best course of action. The first is to take the saw to a professional sharpening service and have them restore the edge. If you are in the middle of a project this choice has little appeal. Your second choice is, of course, to sharpen the handsaw yourself. It is probably safe to say that if you are in a hurry for the saw and have never sharpened a saw in the past, your best bet would be to have a professional do the sharpening. Keep in mind that the chances of ruining a quality saw by improper sharpening are good if you have never attempted the task in the past. You should learn the basics of sharpening a handsaw when you have the time to devote to the learning process. It is also helpful to attempt your first handsaw sharpening on an old and worthless saw. This way, if you should go wrong you will not ruin your best saw.

There are a number of things to be learned by carefully looking over a saw blade before sharpening is attempted. The first part of your inspection should be to see if any teeth are broken or chipped. This can easily happen by hitting a nail or twisting the saw while cutting. Another possible source of damage to the saw might be as a result of rough handling in general—if the handsaw is kept in a large toolbox without some type of sheath over the blade, for example. Whatever the cause, broken or missing teeth will indicate to you that more work will be required for the sharpening.

Jointing

The first step in sharpening a handsaw is called "jointing" and it is a necessary step to make all of the tips of the teeth the same height. If one or more of the teeth are broken or missing, you will have lots of work to do in getting all of the remaining unbroken teeth down to the same level.

The task of jointing a handsaw begins by first fastening the saw (teeth facing upwards) in a suitable vise. You will find it helpful to clamp the saw blade sandwiched between two pieces of lumber (1×6 inches or so) with the teeth protruding about 1½ inches up from the edges of the lumber. This spacing is adequate for most people to work with a file, but if your hands are larger or smaller than most, you might find that increasing or reducing the position of the teeth relative to the lumber will give you a better working height. The only caution that I can offer is that too much working height will not keep the saw blade from moving or chattering, so there is really a limit as to the most acceptable distance.

A professional saw sharpener will use a special tool for jointing a saw blade but there is no need for the do-it-yourselfer to go to the expense. A flat file, when used with a sharp eye, can easily be used for jointing the teeth on a handsaw. Hold the file in both hands with the handle end of the file toward you. The thumbs are held on the file, and the index fingers under the file and pointing toward you. By holding the file in this manner it is easy to keep it at right angles to the sides of the saw. While filing, knuckles ride the "rails," such as they are, on the lumber (Fig. 3-7).

The file is pushed forward lightly over the saw lengthwise as many times as necessary to file all of the high points of the teeth down to the level of the lowest tooth. Some specialized lighting may be of help when jointing a handsaw

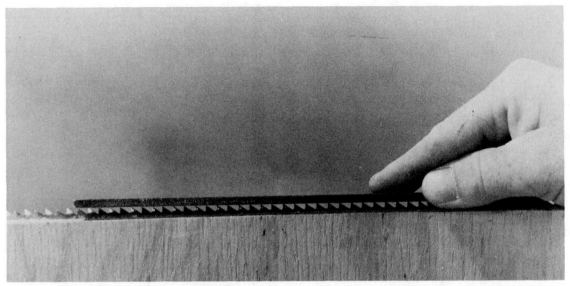

Fig. 3-7. A handsaw can be jointed with a flat file.

with a flat file. By adjusting the lighting so that it shines on the teeth, it will be easy to see when all of the tips of the teeth have been touched by the file. This will appear as a bright flat plane on the top of each tooth. It will be easy to identify those teeth that remain dull after the file has made a few passes. Keep in mind that if any tooth is shorter than the rest, it will not do any cutting as the saw blade is being drawn through a piece of lumber during the cutting process. A tooth such as this is useless. Unless there has been some exceptional damage to one or more of the teeth on the blade, it should not take more than a few passes with the file to render all teeth the same height.

Fitting

The next step in the handsaw sharpening process is technically known as *fitting* the saw, but for simplicity's sake let's refer to this step as *filing*. Since there are two basically different tooth designs—*ripsaw* and *crosscut* saw—we must discuss each separately.

The shape of ripsaw teeth is shown in Fig. 3-8. The front or cutting face of the teeth are at right angles to an imaginary line drawn along the points of the teeth. You can easily check this with a square as shown in Fig. 3-9. A triangular file in the correct position is also shown. It should also be noted that the side of the file which is against the front of a tooth is held plumb. By holding one side of the file plumb and by pressing the file down into the gullet, the back of the tooth will be at a 30-degree angle to a line along the points of the teeth.

Assuming that you are right-handed, hold the handle end of the file firmly; the point of the file is held lightly between the thumb and index finger of the left hand. Every other tooth is

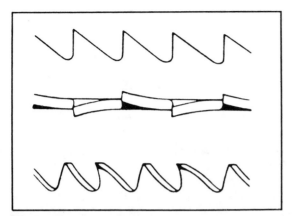

Fig. 3-8. Ripsaw tooth detail.

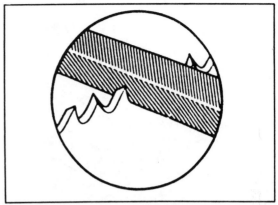

Fig. 3-10. File position for crosscut teeth.

filed from one side of the saw, then the saw is turned end for end, and the rest of the teeth are filed from the other side in the same fashion. At each stroke, the file is to cut the back of the tooth that projects away from you and the front of the adjoining tooth as well. If the teeth are uneven, they should be gradually equalized in size by pressing the file against the larger tooth.

The position of the saw in the file during fitting should be to your advantage. As a rule, the saw is placed in the clamp so that the teeth

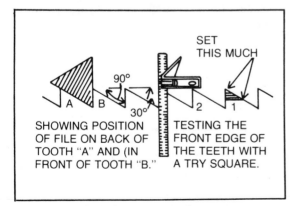

SHOWING POSITION OF FILE ON BACK OF TOOTH "A" AND (IN FRONT OF TOOTH "B." | SET THIS MUCH / TESTING THE FRONT EDGE OF THE TEETH WITH A TRY SQUARE.

Fig. 3-9. Filing angle for crosscut teeth.

protrude above the jaws of the vise by ¼ inch, or, if you are using a 1×6 inch lumber sandwich, only about ½ inch. Keep in mind that unless the saw is placed low, it will vibrate and screech, and the file will not cut well. The file is held straight across the saw, as shown in the illustrations. Since most files cut on the forward stroke only, it should be raised up from the cutting at the end of each stroke and then brought back into sharpening position. Long, light, even strokes of the file are the best way to ensure that the filing is done correctly. It is probably safe to estimate that the average ripsaw tooth can be sharpened with no more than two long strokes of a sharp file (Fig. 3-10).

After a saw is jointed, the teeth are usually uniform. But often one or two will have been filed incorrectly. It is important to scrutinize *each* tooth after you feel the filing is complete. Correct any glaringly wrong teeth before going any further with the sharpening.

The cutting action of a ripsaw is shown in Fig. 3-11. As you can see, the teeth of this blade are really a series of tiny chisels. If all of the teeth are the same size, shape, and height,

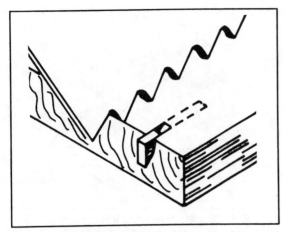

Fig. 3-11. The cutting section of a ripsaw.

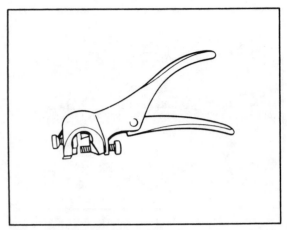

Fig. 3-12. Sawtooth setting tool.

each will cut with a force that is equal to the others and the cutting will go smoothly. Teeth which are not uniform will cause the cutting action to be other than we expected.

Setting a Ripsaw

The final step in the sharpening of a ripsaw is called *setting* and this is done to make the kerf of the saw greater than the thickness of the blade. For a point of reference, a ripsaw that will be used in wet or green wood will operate much more efficiently if the kerf is wide. A ripsaw used on dry lumber, on the other hand, will need only the slightest kerf to cut well. Every other tooth is set to the right, and the rest of the teeth are set to the left. The easiest way of setting saw teeth is with a special tool called a *saw set* (Fig. 3-12). This tool is hand-operated and simply presses individual teeth out to create the kerf. Set the tool so that not more than half of each tooth is set or, in other words, so only the point and not the whole of each tooth is bent. As a point of reference, the shaded part of the tooth numbered 1

in Fig. 3-13 is set to the right and a similar part of the tooth numbered 2 is set to the left and so on alternately, until all of the saw teeth have been set.

Figure 3-14 is an enlarged view of the teeth of a ripsaw. You can easily see that the cutting edge of each tooth is square to the saw blade and that every alternate tooth is set to the right. Once again, remember that wet or green wood requires a ripsaw with a wider kerf than dry wood.

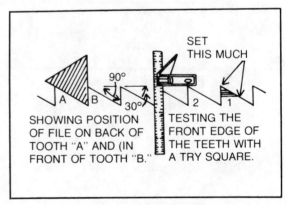

Fig. 3-13. Check tooth angle with tri-square.

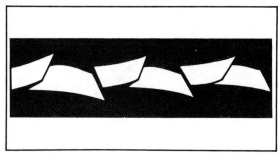
Fig. 3-14. Ripsaw teeth.

Fitting a Crosscut Handsaw

As mentioned earlier, the teeth on a crosscut saw differ somewhat from those on a ripsaw, so they must be sharpened with a different approach. To begin with, crosscut teeth must first be jointed to bring all of the tips of the teeth to the same plane or line, just the same as the teeth of a ripsaw are jointed. The same technique can be used for jointing.

After jointing, the teeth of your crosscut saw may resemble those in Fig. 3-15. Of the four teeth shown, the point of tooth number 1 has just been touched by the file; tooth number 2 was considerably longer and much of the tip has been filed away, leaving a large, flat surface; tooth number 3, as a result of a poor

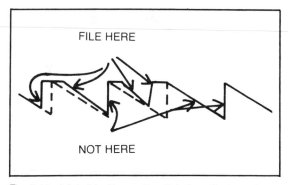
Fig. 3-15. Jointed teeth are often flat along the top edges.

previous filing, was also longer than tooth number 1; and tooth number 4 is larger than any of the others. To file these teeth properly, number 1 is left as is, number 2 is brought to a point by filing against the front edge only, the back of number 3 tooth is filed with the same strokes of the file used for the front of number 2; and number 4 is brought to a point by filing the front and back edges until the metal is filed away to the dotted lines. By using this procedure, all of the teeth are made the same size and shape.

The correct shape of the teeth of a crosscut handsaw is shown in Fig. 3-16. It should be noted that the front or cutting edge of each tooth is not at a right angle to the line of teeth, as the teeth are on a ripsaw. The teeth on a crosscut saw are 12 degrees more than a right angle, or 102 degrees. This incidentally is an industry standard for crosscut saw teeth. If the cutting edges of the teeth were filed at a right angle, the saw would draw into the wood too much and the end result would be a rough cut.

The angle is often referred to by professional sharpeners as the *hook* of the saw. The amount of hook of the teeth is controlled by the extent to which the file is tilted or tipped sidewise toward the point of the saw during filing. If the file were so held as to have its top side horizontal, the front and the back of each tooth would have the same angle. There would not be enough hook to the front of the teeth to cause them to take hold well. Such a saw is spoken of as a *peg-tooth* saw and, as you can easily guess, will not cut well.

The crosscut handsaw is not filed straight across as the ripsaw was previously. The file is held so that the point of the file points toward the handle of the saw, and so that there is an

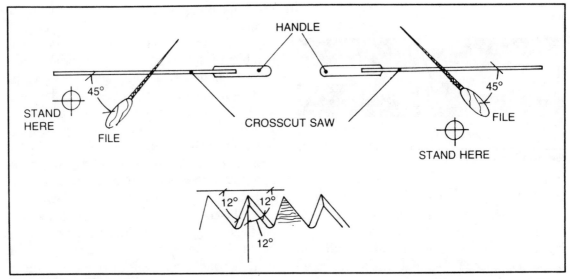

Fig. 3-16. Proper filing action.

angle of 45 degrees between the handle end of the file and the tip end of the saw. The smaller this angle—that is, the closer the handle end of the file is held to the blade of the saw—the keener will be the resulting cutting edges of the teeth. There is a difference of opinion among the experts as to the best or most advantageous way to hold the file. Some of the pros file as in Fig. 3-16., filing against the cutting edges of the teeth. Others file toward the tip of the saw and maintain that the saw takes hold better and makes a smoother cut. The method illustrated is the one used most frequently. The position that the filer should stand at is also indicated in the drawing. The way to hold the file is shown in Fig. 3-16. A filer may begin at either side and at either end and file every other tooth, then turn the saw in the clamp and file all of the missed teeth.

To ensure the best success, file very carefully, stopping often to examine the work in progress. If a watchful eye is kept, it is safe to assume that the filing will result in predictable results.

Ordinarily, saws are set before they are filed, but saws poorly filed in the past may appear as in Fig. 3-17 when they have been jointed. There is so little gullet between teeth 2 and 3 that they cannot be set. As with a

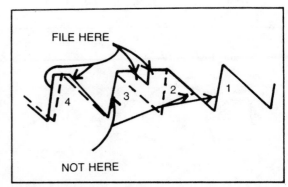

Fig. 3-17. Improperly sharpened saw may need repair; file as described in text.

54

ripsaw, only half of the tooth is set on a crosscut handsaw. The shaded part of the tooth numbered 1 shows the part that is to be bent over. Every other tooth is set to the right and the rest to the left; the clearance which is obtained for the saw blade by the set is shown in Fig. 3-18. The set makes a cut or kerf wider than the thickness of the blade of the saw. The amount of set depends largely on the type of work that will be done with the saw. As a rule, green or wet wood requires more set than dry woods do. For all-around general crosscut use, the saw teeth should be set a little wider than normal. The only possible exception to this is when using a crosscut handsaw for finish cutting of cabinet or other fine woodwork.

To be sure, there are other types of saws around the home workshop than those described above. Generally speaking however, all saws fall into one of two categories—ripsaw or crosscut—so if you are faced with sharpening a saw, approach it from one of these points of reference and you will not go wrong.

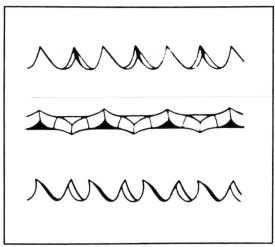

Fig. 3-18. The teeth of a crosscut saw blade.

SHAPING TOOLS

The well-equipped woodworking shop will have a number of hand-powered tools that are used for shaping woodworking projects. Chances are very good that your shop, no matter how small, will contain at least two of these useful tools. A well-rounded collection of these tools will include the following: chisels, gouges, carving tools, plane, scrapers, spokeshave, and drawknife. While there are other hand woodworking tools that help us to shape, the above listing is the most common.

CHISELS

A chisel (Fig. 3-19) works best when razor-sharp. Oddly enough, whenever I inspect a fellow worker's chisel, I find it to be a little on the dull side. I have found it worthwhile to take some time to put a fresh edge on a chisel just prior to use. This way I know it is ready for the task at hand. I will explain how this is done with a stone later in this section.

Another useful habit is to store a chisel in some type of protective sheath when not in use. Most sets of chisels come in a handy plastic package that is intended for storage. Unfortunately, these usually become damaged beyond serviceability rather quickly, and more often than not, the chisels suffer some type of damage. Many professional carpenters will store their chisel sets in a canvas storage roll.

I have been using a chisel storage case for several years now, and I have never had any damage done to the blade of the single (¾ inch) woodworking chisel I carry in my general purpose tool box. My chisel sheath consists of a 9½-inch piece of bamboo. One end of this tube contains the ring or node of the bamboo, and the other end is simply open to receive the

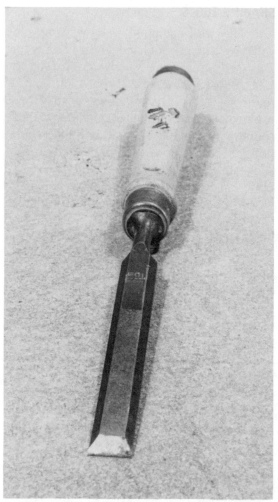

Before use I always touch up the edge of my woodworking chisel. This takes only a few moments but is worth the investment in time, as I can then be certain that I will have a sharp tool to work with. Unless the chisel has been

Fig. 3-19. A good wood chisel will last a lifetime with a little care.

chisel. I have several wraps of tape around the case to hold it together. As I recall, the repair was necessary one day after dropping a crowbar on top of the case with the chisel inside. As it turns out, bamboo is as strong as brass and the chisel was not harmed. I have been planning to make more of these bamboo cases for other tools as well (Fig. 3-20).

Fig. 3-20. Homemade bamboo case for wood chisel.

damaged along the cutting edge, this light sharpening, or touching-up should be all that your chisel needs.

A wood chisel is held at about 35 degrees off the surface of the sharpening stone (Fig. 3-21). Honing oil should be used for the whetting. Three or four forward strokes are made with the chisel held firmly against the stone. The chisel is then placed in a horizontal position, with the flat side on the stone. With three or four forward passes with the stone, the wire edge is removed. This touching up is carried out until the chisel is sharp enough to cut well. In most cases, this will be about five times. A wood chisel is sharp when a cut has a smooth surface. If marks show on the surface of a piece of wood after this test, a few more passes with the oilstone are needed to develop a sharper edge.

As an aid to the casual sharpener, there are a number of aids on the market that can make sharpening a wood chisel and easy task indeed, providing you follow the directions. In most cases, these devices clamp onto the wood chisel and hold it at a predetermined angle to the oilstone. These sharpening aids work well, but if you understand the basics of sharpening a wood chisel, you will be able to do the sharpening without the aid of a special clamp-on device. Since part of the beauty of woodwork-

Fig. 3-21. Sharpening a wood chisel on a benchstone.

Fig. 3-22. A damaged chisel blade will require grinding.

be adjusted so that it is horizontal or 180 degrees off the surface. Then the damaged chisel is placed on the tool rest with the bevel side up, and the cutting edge is ground square to the sides of the chisel and back to the bottom of the chip (or nicks, if they are present). The tool is kept moving right to left so that the wear on the grinding wheel will be even. Next, the tool rest

Fig. 3-23. Grind a chisel with the bevel up.

ing is the simplicity of the work, it is sometimes better to fully understand what is going on so there will be little need for special (and often costly) aids to do something right.

Sooner or later you will probably take a chunk out of the cutting edge of your wood chisel. I have done this while cutting a mortise for a lock in a door jamb and hitting a nail in the process. The only solution to a damaged cutting edge on a wood chisel is to regrind the edge (Fig. 3-22). This is most easily accomplished on a bench grinder with an adjustable tool rest.

The tool rest on the bench grinder should

is adjusted to about 30 degrees and a bevel is ground on one side. Hold the chisel lightly to the grinding wheel, moving it from side to side often. A ¼ inch bevel is suitable for most general types of carpentry work. After you have ground for a few moments—this work goes very quickly—you should remove the tool from the grinder to examine the bevel in progress. If the bevel is too short, you should adjust your technique by lowering the chisel handle, or by holding it up further on the stone. If it is too long, you can raise the handle end or place it lower on the stone. The point of the chisel is dipped in water often to keep the metal cool. Do this often so the metal of the chisel never gets hotter than you can touch without getting burned. Keep in mind that a light touch will produce the kind of sharp tool you are after (Figs. 3-23 through 3-25).

The grinding continues until the edge is turned and a wire edge is produced. This can be observed by looking carefully at the end of the

Fig. 3-24. Reset the tool rest to grind the bevel at 30 degrees.

Fig. 3-25. Dip the chisel in water to keep the temperature of the steel down.

chisel, or by drawing the flat side across the palm of the hand. If it is smooth, it is an indication that the edge has not been turned. The turned edge will slightly scratch the hand when sharp.

The next step in sharpening a damaged chisel is to work on an oilstone as described earlier. This is done resulting in a chisel with a 35 degree bevel which is suitable for most general types of woodworking.

PLANES

It has been suggested that the plane is the aristocrat of woodworking tools. Of all the basic tools, the plane is probably the most misunderstood and complicated. When sharpened properly (which you will learn how to do in this section), a plane is a beautiful tool to work with. But when a plane is dull or maladjusted, it is a definite source of frustration.

When using a plane, you must adjust the depth of cut carefully. Planes are not designed to remove great amounts of wood. Instead, they cut thin, even shavings from the surface. Never use a plane on wood that has nails present, as you will surely do damage to the blade. Another way to dull or ruin a good plane blade is to use the plane for removing dried glue or old, heavy paint. The proper tools for removing these coatings are paint scrapers and sanders.

When you are finished working with a plane, lay it on its side rather than flat. This way the tool will not rest on its cutting blade. You should also store your plane in a safe place so it will not become damaged by other tools.

As a rule, the woodworking plane blade is sharpened in a manner similar to a woodworking chisel. That is, unless there has been some damage to the cutting edge, the plane blade is touched up on a whetstone to an angle of about 35 degrees. Use plenty of honing oil and move the blade in either an oval or figure-eight movement. Stop often, wipe the oil off the end of the blade, and inspect the honing. What you should be looking for is the wire edge that will be formed along the back of the blade. More often than not you will be able to feel this wire before you can see it. Lightly rub your finger over the flat of the blade. The wire edge indicates that the work on the oilstone is almost complete. When the wire appears, break it off by running the blade across the edge grain of a piece of hardwood. White oak is a good choice. Then whet the edge lightly once again. The last step is to turn the blade over and give the flat side a few light rubs with the stone. It is very important that this side of the plane blade be held absolutely flat against the stone. After this has been done, the blade of the plane should be sharp as a razor and ready to be reinstalled inside the plane body.

If the woodworking plane blade has been damaged it must be reconditioned in a manner that is similar to that used for the wood chisel described earlier. Because the blade of a wood plane is wide—much wider than the average woodworking chisel—some type of guide is necessary for grinding. Often the tool rest on your bench grinder can be used to good advantage.

Begin by adjusting the tool rest so it is horizontal. Next, lay the blade of the plane on the tool rest with the bevel side up and make contact with the spinning grinding wheel. Move the blade back and forth constantly when grinding, while at the same time keeping it flat on the tool rest. Stop often to check the progress of the grinding and to make certain that the blade is not becoming too hot. Keep a can of water close by when grinding; dip the plane blade into the water often to keep it cool. Check the blade with a try square to determine when the end has been ground to a perfect 90 degree angle (Figs. 3-26, 3-27).

After the tip of the wood plane has been ground square, the next step is to grind a new bevel. As with a wood chisel, the bevel on a plane is about 30 degrees. Adjust the tool rest on the bench grinder to this angle and begin grinding the end of the wood plane. It takes a little practice to be able to hold a wide plane blade against a grinding wheel, so work carefully. Stop often to check on the grinding and also to keep the blade cool (Fig. 3-28).

Once the 30 degree bevel has been ground on the wheel, it is time to begin work on the whetstone to achieve a sharp bevel edge of

approximately 35 degrees. Since the plane blade is wide, it is difficult for the amateur to whet it on a stone with total accuracy. In this instance, I would recommend that you use some type of guidance system for the whetting. There are a number of these available and it may be worth your while to invest in one. In any event, the bevel edge of the woodworking plane must be worked on the well-oiled stone

Fig. 3-26. Grinding a wood plane blade off square.

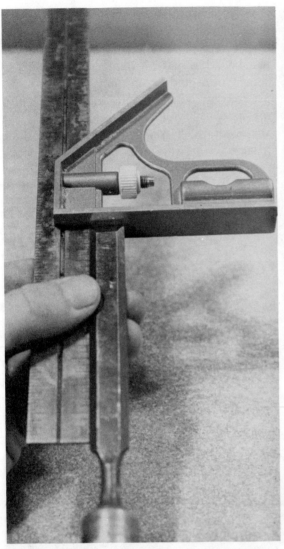

Fig. 3-27. Check the squareness of a blade will a tri-square.

Fig. 3-28. Grinding the edge bevel on a wood chisel.

until a sharp 35 degree angle is achieved. Next, turn the plane blade over and give the flat side a few swipes. It is important that the blade be held absolutely flat for this. Check the sharpness of the blade; when it is razor sharp, reinstall it in the plane body and adjust the depth of cut. Remember that your woodworking plane will stay sharp longer if it is used to remove only slight amounts of surface material.

DRAWKNIVES

These days, one is more likely to see a drawknife (Fig. 3-29) on the wall being used as a decoration rather than in active service. Now the work that was done by the drawknife in the past is quickly accomplished by more modern power tools such as jointer/planer and lathe. Nevertheless, there are still a few who remember not only how to use this tool but also for what.

The proper way to sharpen a drawknife (sometimes called a *drawshave*) begins with a careful inspection of the cutting edge. If nicks, gouges, or other blemishes are present on the cutting edge, the unit must be reground before sharpening can begin, and the grinding must go

to a point just beyond the depth of the damage.

Before grinding, you must first adjust the tool rest on your bench grinder so that it will be of value when grinding. The proper adjustment for this initial grinding is to the horizontal. Once this has been accomplished, turn on the grinder and begin grinding the edge of the drawknife until the edge is free from nicks, etc. and square. The drawknife is held with the bevel up during this grinding. As with other grinding, do not let the metal of the drawknife get too hot to touch. A can of water or a plant atomizer filled with water should be used to keep the blade cool.

After the edge of the drawknife has been cleaned of blemishes, you must next regrind

Fig. 3-29. Draw knife.

the bevel. Adjust the tool rest accordingly and have a go at creating this bevel angle on the cutting edge of the drawknife. Work carefully and stop often to check on the progress. Keep the blade cool. In a short while, you should have the bevel ground. The next step is to work with an oilstone to finish the sharpening. As a rule, a flat oilstone is better for this work than a whetstone. The oilstone is held flat on the flat side of the drawknife and the wire edge is removed. The tool is then held with one end under the left shoulder and the stone is used to produce another bevel shorter than the one made by the grinder—say, about 35 degrees. Work carefully and keep a sharp eye on the angle of the bevel you are recreating.

SCRAPERS

A number of different types of scrapers (Fig. 3-33) can be found around the home woodworking shop. There is, of course, the traditional scraper, which resembles a very small drawknife, and there are also paint scrapers of several different varieties. As a

Fig. 3-30. These are all considered scrapers.

rule, all scrapers operate by removing a thin layer of material from the surface of the work. Where there are differences between types of scrapers, they are generally along the lines of whether the unit is pulled or pushed across the surface of the work.

Generally, a scraper that is *pulled* across the surface will have a beveled edge—usually around 45 degrees. On the other hand, scrapers that are *pushed* across the work surface commonly have a leading edge which is at a right angle to the blade (Fig. 3-31).

The size of the tool will have some bearing on the method used to sharpen the scraper. Small scrapers can usually be sharpened quite easily with the aid of a good file, while larger scrapers can be touched up quicker on a bench grinder. If the edge of the scraper is damaged (no matter what the bevel), it will have to be

ground to a point just beyond the damage. This is most easily done on a bench grinder.

For scrapers with a flat edge, I find a file to be most useful for restoring the squareness. Probably the best example of a square-edge scraper is a paint scraper or putty knife. Most do-it-yourselfers do not know that a paint scraper has a square edge, and as a result actually sharpen this tool. Not only is this a waste of time (for this is not an easy task), but a paint scraper so sharpened will have a definite tendency to gouge the surface rather than take a layer of paint off. For future reference, the proper edge on a paint scraper—as shown in Fig. 3-32—is 90 degrees.

Probably the easiest way to put a square edge back on a paint scraper is to lay a file on the work bench or clamp it horizontal in a good vise. Next, with two hands, work the scraper

Fig. 3-31. Flat edge scraper (left) and beveled edge scraper.

Fig. 3-32. File the edge of a scraper off at 90 degrees.

over the file. It is important that the hands hold the scraper at a perfect 90 degree angle to the surface of the file. Of course if the blade was damaged to begin with, it will have first been ground on a bench grinder, then worked with the file to achieve a 90 degree angle edge.

Scrapers that have a beveled edge can be sharpened with either bench grinder or file. Of course, if damage is present to the cutting edge of this type of scraper, it must be ground past the damage and a new bevel then ground. If you find that grinding is necessary, work carefully and do not allow the metal to get too hot to touch. Use the tool grinding guide to help you grind the scraper blade to a 90 degree angle and then to the proper 35 degree finish edge. Generally speaking, a scraper blade need not be worked with a whetstone for this would give a sharp edge which is not correct for this type of tool (Fig. 3-33).

BORING TOOLS

Common tools in this, the smallest grouping, help us to make holes in all types of material including wood, plastic, metal, and other modern materials. While there are several different tools, all fall into one of two broad groups best exemplified by the *awl* and *auger bit*. As with other handtools in this chapter, the two groups represent different types of cutting or boring edges and therefore are best discussed within these parameters (Fig. 3-34).

AWL-LIKE TOOLS

The distinguishing characteristic of this group of hand tools is the tip of the tool, which is always tapered to a sharp point. As with any guideline there are exceptions, including a nail set which has a flat tip although the shaft of the tool is tapered. Nevertheless, awl-like handtools are all sharpened in a similar manner (Fig. 3-35).

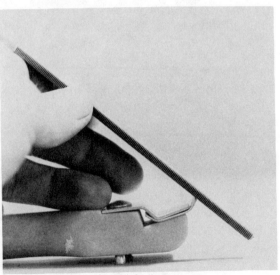

Fig. 3-33. File this scraper off at 35 degrees.

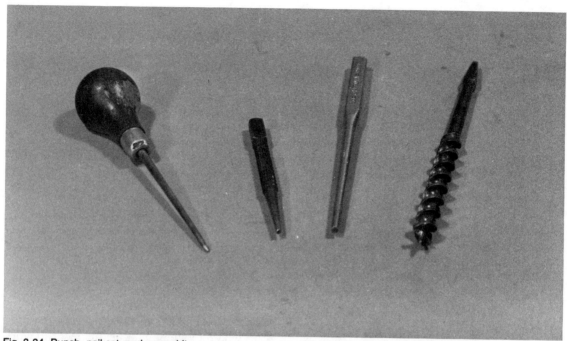

Fig. 3-34. Punch, nail set, and auger bit.

As with any sharpening task, the first step is to carefully look over the tool to determine just how much work needs to be done. Since awl-like hand tools are commonly used in conjunction with a hammer, the head of the tool must be inspected for mushrooming. If the tool has seen a lot of service, its head will probably be mushroomed over and this must be reground during the sharpening process. Your task is to restore the original bevel to the head of the tool and this is most easily accomplished by holding it against a bench grinder. Adjust the tool rest to the best advantage and remove all mushroomed metal from the head (Fig. 3-36).

The next step is to sharpen the point on the tool—unless, of course, the tip of the tool is flat, in which case it will be ground to a 90

Fig. 3-35. The awl is pointed while the nail set has a flat tip.

Fig. 3-36. A mushroomed head on a nail set is dangerous and should be removed.

have two flat surfaces on opposite sides of the point. The next two grinds should be done so that when finished you have ground four flat sides forming a point on the end of the tool. Keep in mind that the tip of the tool should never become too hot to touch. To prevent this, dip the tool into cool water after each of the four sides have been ground. The end result should be a four-sided point (Fig. 3-37).

To achieve a cone-shaped point on an awl-like tool, you will find a whetstone helpful. First apply a few drops of oil to the surface of the stone, then turn the tool between the fingers while at the same time stroking it along the stone, the shaft being held and tilted up to form the desired point angle. Keep turning the tool so that the point will remain in the center of the tool. If, for example, you were to stroke several times without twisting the tool, the point would move off center. Inspect the work often. When the desired point is achieved, wipe off the oil and the tool is ready for service (Fig. 3-38).

Awl-like tools with a flat point—such as the nail set—are most easily reconditioned on

degree angle to the shaft. Look at the tip of the tool carefully and determine if the point is four-sided or cone-shaped. A four-sided point is most easily made with a bench grinder while a cone-shaped point is achieved on a whetstone.

The four-sided point is most easily developed on a bench grinder. First adjust the tool rest (with the bench grinder off) so that when the shaft of the tool is rested on it, the angle of the grind will be approximately 35 degrees. Next turn the bench grinder on, and once the spinning wheel has reached maximum rpm, lay the tool on the guide so that the tip just comes in contact with the wheel. Grind for a few moments, then remove the tool from the tool rest. Now turn the tool over so that the first grind is on top and grind the opposite side of the point, remove the tool and you should

Fig. 3-37. Four-sided tip on tool.

a bench grinder. Begin by inspecting the tip for damage, as this will determine how much grinding is required. Next, adjust the tool guide on the bench grinder so that it is on a plane of 90 degrees from the grinding wheel. Use the tool as a guide for this because due to the tapered shaft, the tool grinding guide must be adjusted so that when the tool rests on the guide, the end will be at a 90 degree angle to the grinding wheel (Fig. 3-39).

As with other grinding, the tool should not be allowed to become too hot to touch as this would take the temper out of the steel. To prevent overheating, dip the tool in cool water often. It is also important to turn the tool between your fingers while grinding, as this will help you to achieve a flat tip. After a few moments of grinding, check the tip carefully. Often a burr or slight mushrooming will result, especially if you are pushing the tool firmly into the spinning wheel. If this occurs, regrind the shaft of the tool slightly to remove the burr.

AUGER BITS

Auger bits are used only in the hand-powered brace, *never* in an electric drill, as these tools spin too quickly for the auger bit to bore effectively. When an auger bit is sharp, it

Fig. 3-38. Develop a round tip on an oilstone by twisting the tool between the fingers while sharpening.

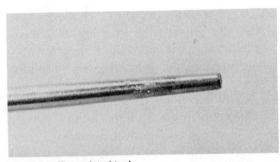

Fig. 3-39. Flat pointed tool.

is very easy to use and will help you to bore a clean hole, the size of which is determined by the diameter of the bit itself. An auger bit should last a lifetime with just a minimum of care in the form of keeping it lightly oiled to prevent rust and touching up the cutting edge as often as required.

If upon inspection of your auger bit you discover rust, you should remove it as quickly as possible. An old carpenter's trick works well for removing rust so I will pass it along to you. A strand of rope, saturated in motor oil and then coated with valve grinding compound or emery dust, is very useful for removing rust from inside the grooves on most auger bits—smaller bits will require thinner rope or string but use the same basic principle. Begin by clamping the rusted auger bit in a sturdy bench vise. The rope is wound once or twice around the bit and drawn back and forth. The oil holds the emery dust (or valve grinding compound) on the rope and the dust acts as an abrasive which cleans the rust from the metal (Fig. 3-40). A good way to coat the rope with the emery dust is to put about two tablespoonsful of the dust in a dish, add the length of rope (about 12 to 15 inches should be plenty) then cover with motor oil. Mix thoroughly with a

stick and both the oil and emery dust will saturate the rope.

An auger bit is sharpened with either a triangular or a thin flat file. As a rule, large auger bits can be sharpened with either type of file but smaller bits are easier to touch up or sharpen with a triangular file.

To file an auger bit, begin by placing it on a bench or table horizontally and lightly file off the parts of the spur which have been bent outward. This is done by holding the file as shown in (Fig. 3-41). Care must be exercised here to keep the edges their approximate diameter all around. Keep the file laying flat and it will only remove bent or curled metal.

The next step is to file the spur to a sharp edge. This is done by holding the bit as in Fig. 3-42 and filing only the inside of the spur at the front or cutting edge. The filing angle is impor-

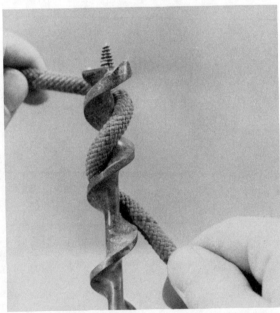

Fig. 3-40. Use a rope soaked in oil to clean an auger bit.

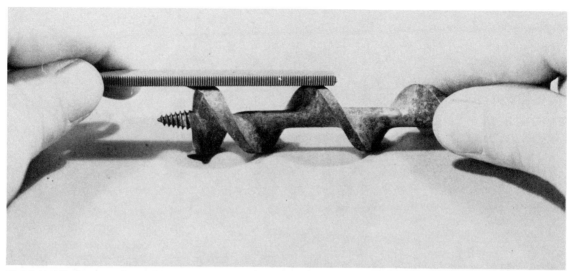

Fig. 3-41. File the spur of an auger bit with a flat file.

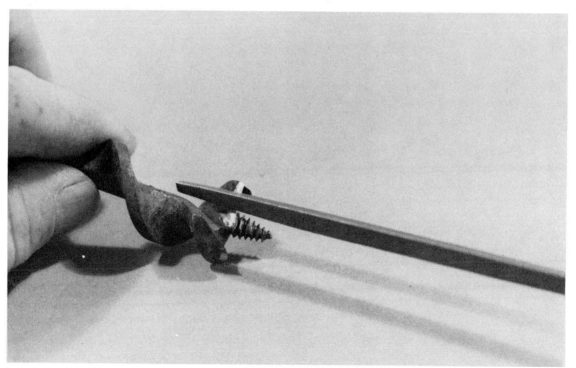

Fig. 3-42. File an auger bit in this manner.

Fig. 3-43. Spray silicone will prevent rust on any tool.

tant and you should strive to duplicate the original edge with the file. If you are in doubt as to the proper angle, you will find it helpful to examine a new auger bit. Exercise care when working so you do not undercut the screw point where it joins the cutting edges of the auger bit. File a bevel edge on both cutting edges and make certain that they are equal or one will cut

more than the other. Some carpenters like to further sharpen with a whetstone after filing to develop an even keener edge.

Finally, apply a light coat of oil to the auger bit (Fig. 3-43). Almost any spray lubricant is useful for this, or use engine oil instead. Store your sharpened auger bit in a special hard case, or in a roll if available.

Chapter 4

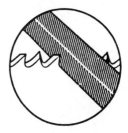

Power Woodworking Tools

The typical home woodworking shop will contain a variety of power tools—in most cases, more power tools than hand tools. Just take a casual glance around the average homeowner's workshop and you're likely to see a hand-held circular saw, table saw, radial arm saw, band saw, saber saw, router, jointer/planer, and hand-held electrical drill. More adventurous woodworkers may have additional tools. In some cases, many of these tools are combined to form one of the big shop machines such as the ShopSmith Mark V (Fig. 4-1). In other cases, there will be a collection of different tools, each capable of, for example, sawing lumber in one manner or another. It would be very costly indeed if the owner of such equipment had to buy or have sharpened all of the cutting edges on these tools. The current cost of sharpening one circular saw blade (7½ in-

ches in diameter) is around $8. Depending on the wood species being cut, this same saw blade can be expected to give from one to eight hours of service.

Because of the popularity of electrical power tools, it is necessary to learn how to sharpen the various cutting edges so that maximum performance can be achieved at all times. It should also be noted that a power tool with a less than razor sharp cutting edge will labor unnecessarily when being used and, as a result, will have a shorter engine life. Still another good reason for using only properly-sharpened cutting edges on power tools is that less than perfect cuts will result from a dull tool.

For ease of discussion, this chapter will be divided into three sections, each of which will deal with a specific type of cutting edge.

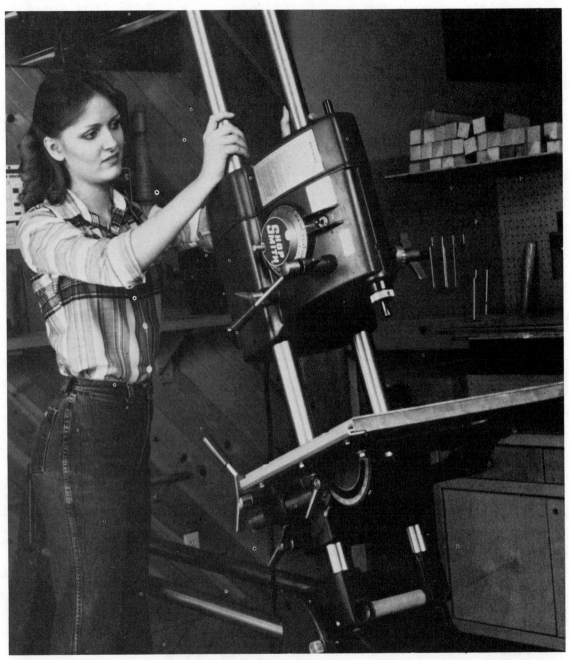

Fig. 4-1. The ShopSmith Mark V is a workshop in itself (ShopSmith).

These main sections are saw blades, shaping tools, and boring tools. Any power tool in the home workshop will fall into one of these large groupings (Fig. 4-2).

POWER SAW BLADES

In this, the largest grouping of power tools, we would obviously find hand-held circular saws, table and radial arm saws, saber saws, and band saws. Since the procedures for sharpening circular saw blades—as used in hand-held circular, table, and radial arm saws are the same, we will discuss how to sharpen these types of blades as if all circular saw blades were interchangeable (which, in some cases, they are). The other types of saw blades will be discussed individually.

Circular Saw Blades

Before we can begin discussing how to sharpen circular saw blades, we first need to take a look at the different types. While all circular saw blades are sharpened in a similar manner, there are some filing tasks that are necessary on some blades and not on others. Let's take a brief look at the more popular types of circular saw blades before we get into the nuts and bolts of sharpening.

Combination circular saw blades are so named because they will crosscut, mitre, and rip. Most manufacturers offer four types of combination circular saw blades: the *all-purpose* (which is flat ground) for smooth cutting in any direction through all types of wood; the *chisel tooth* (also flat ground) for fast, rugged

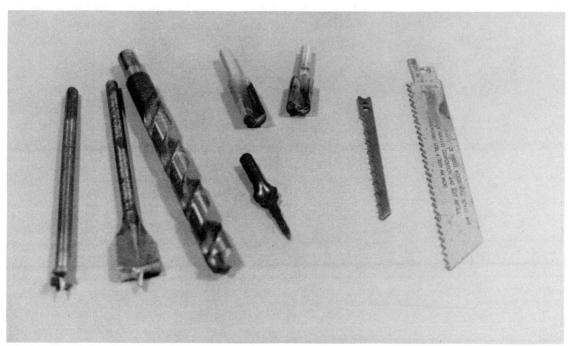

Fig. 4-2. Almost all cutting edges of power tools can be sharpened.

general types of cuts; the *planer* (flat ground) with fast-cutting teeth which are set for wider clearance; and the *planer II* (hollow ground) for fast and exceptionally smooth cutting. This last circular saw blade is ideal for furniture and cabinet work with teeth that are hollow ground for clearance (Fig. 4-3).

Rip circular saw blades, as the name implies, are used for making rip cuts in both hard and soft woods. They are commonly filed square to cut wood with the grain; as a result, are not recommended for crosscutting lumber. The teeth on a rip circular saw blade are shaped like tiny chisels and cut chips in a similar manner. One popular variation of the standard rip circular saw blade is called the

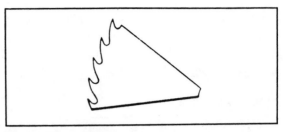

Fig. 4-4. Ripsaw blade.

framing/rip blade and it is used for cutting dimensional lumber—2×4 and 2×6 lumber—during construction of a home. These blades, while not true rip in design, produce acceptable cuts in lumber and, of possible greater importance, do the cutting very quickly (Fig. 4-4).

Plywood circular saw blades are suitable only for cutting plywood, hence the name. Plywood blades are available in both flat ground and hollow ground versions. The flat ground blade allows for smooth cutting of plywood paneling, plywood, and laminates and can cope with situations where some nails may be present such as old flooring. The hollow ground plywood circular saw blade is generally considered the top-of-the-line blade for plywood. It has bevelled teeth and allows virtually splinter-free cutting. The hollow ground plywood blade is used extensively in the building of plywood furniture largely due to the smooth cuts that it produces (Fig. 4-5).

Carbide-tipped blades offer a cutting performance that lasts up to 15 times as long as conventional steel-toothed circular saw blades. While there are a number of different types of carbide-tipped circular saw blades used for different cutting applications, a good general rule to follow is: the more carbide teeth on a blade, the smoother the finished cut

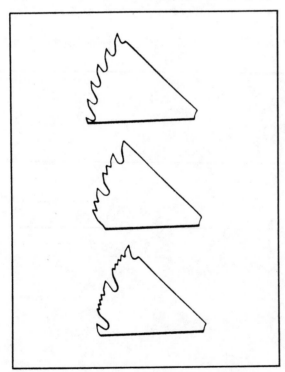

Fig. 4-3. Combination circular saw blade.

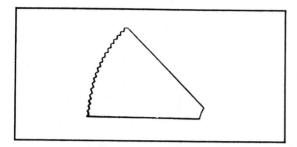

Fig. 4-5. Plywood circular saw blade.

will be. Currently available are eight and ten tooth carbide blades which are suitable for rough, framing types of cuts (Fig. 4-6). Carbide-tipped blades with more teeth—up to 60 teeth per blade—are more suitable for finished cuts on all types of wood. As an example, a cabinet shop will probably have a 60-toothed carbide blade for making finish cuts. The long cutting life of carbide-tipped blades can be directly attributed to the pieces of carbide which are welded to the cutting edges of a circular saw blade. Carbide is so hard that it cannot be sharpened with a conventional file, as all other circular saw blades can. Sharpening carbide cutters requires a special diamond file or diamond file or diamond chip abrasive blade. Since these special tools are not likely to be in the average woodworking shop, we will not discuss how to sharpen carbide-tipped circular

saw blades in this book. It is advisable, therefore, to have carbide-tipped circular saw blades professionally sharpened. This service is not very expensive and can only be done with special tools, as mentioned.

To be sure, there are other types of circular saw blades. Some can be sharpened (such as dado blades), while others do not lend themselves to being touched up—abrasive masonry and tile-cutting blades for instance. Generally speaking, if the blade has teeth which can be ground with a standard file, then it is safe to say it can be sharpened by home methods. Read on through this chapter and you will learn the general procedures that may be required and apply them as necessary (Fig. 4-7).

The first step in the sharpening process for circular saw blades is the realization that your saw is not making cuts as it should. Work will have to be pushed into the saw with greater amounts of pressure which in turn will cause a decided drop in engine rpm and, often as not, will also result in a cut you are not pleased with. At about this time you will make an inspection of the saw blade and probably discover that it is coated with wood gum. It will also probably be black. These are definite signs of a saw blade that has seen some service and it will greatly benefit from a sharpening.

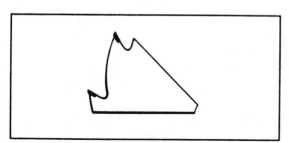

Fig. 4-6. Carbide-tipped circular saw blade.

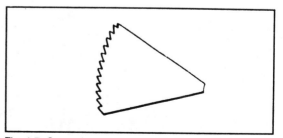

Fig. 4-7. General purpose cutoff circular saw blade.

There are four separate steps to the sharpening process for circular saw blades which are flat ground. These are (in order of procedure): *jointing, gumming, setting,* and *filing.* Circular saw blades which are hollow ground are sharpened in three distinct operations: *rounding, gumming,* and *filing.* You should know from the outset that some aids will make these sharpening operations easier to accomplish and it may therefore be helpful to mention them in passing.

Jointing is an operation where all of the teeth are ground to the same height. This operation is most easy to accomplish on a standard table saw or radial arm saw. For hand-held circular saws, one must accomplish this operation by adjusting the saw table so that the tips of the blade just nick the stone. Once you have a clear understanding of how to joint a circular saw blade, you will be able to make adjustments to a hand-held saw with a sense of purpose. Just remember to disconnect the unit from the power source before beginning.

Since a table saw is the easiest aid for jointing, we will carry on this discussion using one in the demonstration. Begin by first unplugging the table saw for safety's sake. Next, run the blade up (or table down, as the case may be) so that several inches of the blade are exposed. Then check the squareness of the blade with a framing square. Strive for a perfect 90 degree angle by making suitable adjustments (Fig. 4-8).

Adjust the height of the saw blade so that

Fig. 4-8. Adjust table saw blade to 90 degrees angle with square.

it now extends above the table only a fraction of an inch. Lay a piece of scrap lumber on the table and adjust the blade so that all teeth lightly touch the underside. Now you must use a large carborundum stone in place of the lumber and spin the blade once again. The object here is to make all of the teeth the same height without grinding off too much. Of course, if one or more of the teeth have been damaged, then all of the teeth on the blade must be ground down to equal this height. This just might be the time you consider buying a new blade or having the old one ground by a professional. In most cases, jointing is a simple process (Fig. 4-9).

Some experts recommend jointing the saw blade with the electric motor running. While I do not recommend this for your first attempt at jointing, I think it is a worthwhile approach once you have a fair understanding of the procedure involved. Jointing is often done with the blade reversed in the saw and spun backwards, and this method reduces the potential for damage to either the stone or blade. One last tip worth mentioning is that applying lampblack to the tip of each tooth prior to jointing will enable you to see when each tooth has touched the stone. Lighting from the side also helps to see when the carbon has been scraped off each tooth.

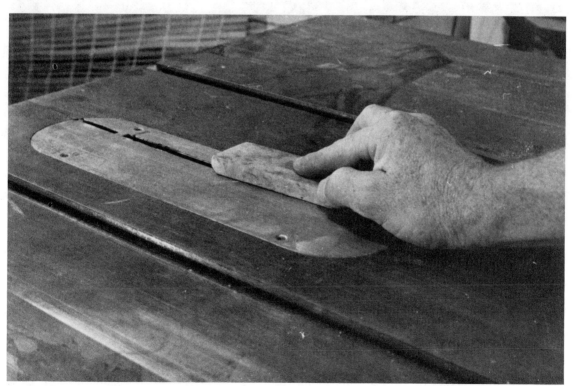

Fig. 4-9. Joint the saw blade with a stone.

Fig. 4-10. Mark just below gullets with pencil.

After you are satisfied that the circular saw blade has been sufficiently jointed, then you must readjust the saw blade so that the gullets are in a position to be filed.

Gumming is the second sharpening operation for circular saw blades and can be done with a round file. A 7/32 inch chain saw file works well for this. If you have the specialized equipment this operation is easier to accomplish, but can be done with care and a good file. Begin by adjusting the saw table so that the gullet of each tooth just clears the table top. Then, with a pencil held in position—just touching a point below each gullet—spin the blade and draw a perfect circle around the blade (Fig. 4-10). After the circle is complete, remove the pencil and raise the blade into a comfortable filing position. Now slowly turn the blade once again and note where each gullet is in relationship to the line. Each should be an equal distance from the circle. The next step involves filling each of the gullets so that they are all as deep as the pencil line circle.

The gumming operation restores the teeth to their correct height when they have been worn shallow by repeated sharpening. It is therefore not necessary to gum a saw every time it is sharpened. As a rule, a circular saw blade should be gummed after every third or fourth sharpening.

When gumming a circular saw blade with a chain saw file, it is important that you do not work any gullet too long. To do so would cause a gullet to heat up beyond temper, resulting in bluing and, in time, a fracture in the area. While the danger of heating up a gullet is ever-present when working on a grinding wheel, the chances of this happening with a file are much less likely. Push the file through the gullet, turning it slightly on each pass. Simply deepen the gullet to the pencil line while at the same time keeping the gullet the same in other respects. Do not, for example, file the sides of the gullet. Instead file the bottom of the gullet itself. You may find it helpful to file only half-way down on each gullet on the first pass. Then on a second pass deepen the gullet to the line. After all of the gullets have been so deepened, you must remove the saw blade from the table saw (or from the hand-held circular saw, if that is what you are using) for the third operation in sharpening.

Setting the teeth on a circular saw is the next step in the sharpening process. Setting the saw means bending the teeth alternately right and left to provide clearance. If the teeth

Fig. 4-11. File gullets with round chain saw file.

are not accurately set, more strain is placed on some teeth than others which can cause them to crack or (in extreme cases) break off. Unevenly set teeth may also cause the saw to chatter as it cuts through work and will most commonly result in a ragged and rough cut.

A circular saw blade which has little set will bind or jam in the cut simply because there is not enough room for the waste wood to be thrown out of the cut. If the teeth are set more on one side than the other, the saw will wander to the side of the heaviest set and breakage of the teeth will soon occur. As you can see, proper set is important for efficient circular saw operation so it must be done with care (Fig. 4-11).

Generally speaking, there are two approaches to the setting operation for a circular saw blade. These two methods are *stake and anvil*, and with a special saw setting tool (Fig. 4-12). Many do-it-yourselfers like the stake and anvil method but bear in mind that this rather specialized tool must be either made or purchased. See Fig. 4-13 for set-up of anvil.

If the anvil and stake is used, the saw should be placed on the stake and the bevelled anvil adjusted to give the required set. The teeth are then set using a hammer and ensuring that the set of each individual tooth does not

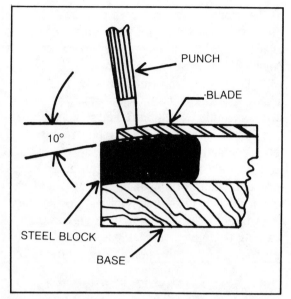

Fig. 4-13. A professional saw setting anvil.

extend more than one quarter of the depth down the tooth.

Circular saw teeth can also be set with the use of a special tool designed for the purpose. Special combination tools for sawtooth setting come with a gauge attachment to regulate the set and special slots graduated to give the desired depth to the set. When placing this tool on the saw, it should be allowed to drop until the point of the saw tooth touches the bottom of the slot. The tooth can then be bent until the gauge touches the side of the blade.

Filing is the last operation in the sharpening process for circular saw blades and is done with the saw blade mounted between two wooden blocks and held tightly in a bench vise (Fig. 4-14). Since the bevels on the cutting teeth will vary with each type (a rip saw blade being different from a combination blade, for example), this is the operation where you must

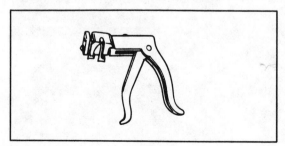

Fig. 4-12. Set sawteeth with this tool.

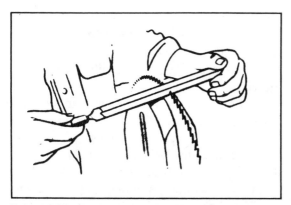

Fig. 4-14. File the teeth of the saw while it is held in a bench vise.

take special care. As general guidelines, a slim taper file is good for sharpening combination blade teeth, while a flat file is used on the rakers. While different saw blades require different filing angles, the basic techniques are the same. Let's now take a look at how to sharpen a few different types of circular saw blade designs.

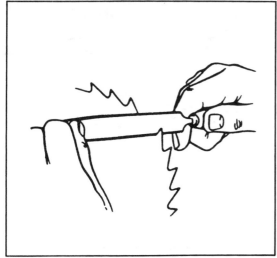

Fig. 4-15. Filing the teeth of a ripsaw.

To file a rip saw, use an eight inch long mill bastard file with two round edges and file straight across the outside edge of the teeth in the direction of the saw set (Fig. 4-15). This means filing alternate teeth, then turning the saw in the vise before filing the remainder. A swivel head vise saves lots of time when filing as the blade does not have to be removed to file alternate teeth—simply swivel the vise instead. Extreme care must be taken to maintain the original hook, shape, and angle of each tooth. If you are in doubt as to the proper angle of the bevel you can check a new, unused blade (if one is around the shop) or possibly consult the manufacturer of the blade. Finish off sharpening by checking the hook of each tooth and rounding the gullets.

Filing cutoff saws—a plywood blade, for example—requires a similar approach except that a thin taper file is used for the operation. Select a taper file to suit the size of the teeth and take care to maintain the original bevel and angle of each tooth. The teeth should be of uniform width and shape and the gullets of equal depth and width. (Note that gullets in this type of saw blade tend to be shallow in depth.) Every tooth should have the same amount of bevel which is most commonly about 12 to 15 degrees, being shorter for soft wood and longer for the harder woods.

File both faces of each tooth to bring it to a point but do not continue any further since this will shorten the teeth (Fig. 4-16). Finish the sharpening by rounding out the gullets with a suitable round and narrow file.

When a planer saw blade is being sharpened, still another technique is used for the process. The raker teeth should be filed first with the aid of a raker gauge which ensures that

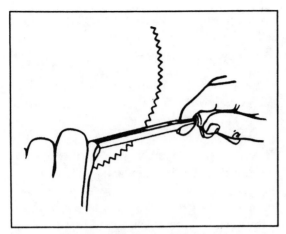

Fig. 4-16. Filing the teeth of a cutoff blade.

the rakers are kept at the recommended depth below the cutting teeth. As a rule, raker teeth are commonly 1/64 inch below the cutting teeth (Fig. 4-17).

If you have a set of dado blade cutters—or dado head as this setup is usually called—you will know when they need sharpening as the quality of the dado will not be uniform. Since sharpening a dado head requires more specialized equipment than the average home workshop will usually contain, it is recommended that you have your dado head sharpened by a professional saw sharpening service. It is important to bear in mind that a blunt dado head can be a hazard to work with because of the nature of the cutting this blade is expected to perform.

Sharpening a circular saw blade is not difficult but it does require your fullest attention during all four sharpening operations. Work carefully and you should be able to restore a circular saw blade with just a bit of effort. Keep in mind that the average charge for sharpening a standard blade—that is, other

than carbide-tipped or dado head—is around six to eight dollars. It is therefore possible to realize such a savings many times a year simply by doing all but the most difficult sharpening yourself.

After you have sharpened a circular saw blade, chances are very good that you will want to press it into service as soon as possible. Once the blade has been reinstalled in the saw, it is wise to give it a light shot of a silicone spray. This will not only help to prevent surface rust but will also lubricate it during the cutting and thus keep it running cooler. This translates into a longer life for the sharpening and you will be surprised at how long it will continue to perform well. If you are not planning to use the blade right away, you should give it a light coating of silicone spray and wrap it in a protective covering (Fig. 4-18). The package the blade came in is a good storage wrapper. Store unused circular saw blades in a

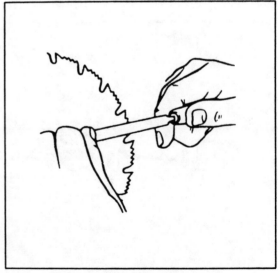

Fig. 4-17. Filing the teeth of a planer saw blade.

Fig. 4-18. Spray circular saw blades with a silicone spray.

safe place to keep them sharp and ready for service.

Reciprocating Saw Blades

Power tools in this grouping include the ever-popular saber saw—the first saw most do-it-yourselfers buy and, according to industry statistics, the biggest selling saw of all—and the more rugged and heavy duty reciprocating action saw. The major differences between these two saws are in power and cutting length. The standard homeowner's saw will generally not have a depth of cut much more than about two inches, while the second type will often have a blade of six to eight inches in length (Fig. 4-19).

Sharpening all types of reciprocating saw blades is approached in the same manner, with a suitable three-sided slim taper file. It is important to choose a file that is not too wide for

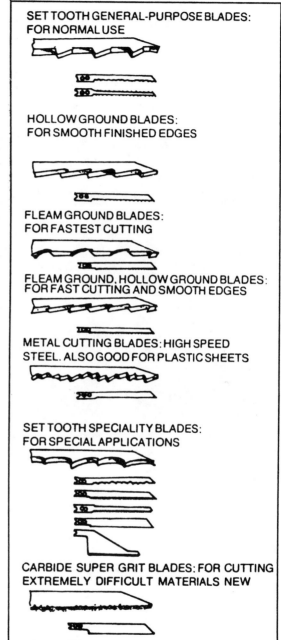

SET TOOTH GENERAL-PURPOSE BLADES: FOR NORMAL USE

HOLLOW GROUND BLADES: FOR SMOOTH FINISHED EDGES

FLEAM GROUND BLADES: FOR FASTEST CUTTING

FLEAM GROUND, HOLLOW GROUND BLADES: FOR FAST CUTTING AND SMOOTH EDGES

METAL CUTTING BLADES: HIGH SPEED STEEL. ALSO GOOD FOR PLASTIC SHEETS

SET TOOTH SPECIALITY BLADES: FOR SPECIAL APPLICATIONS

CARBIDE SUPER GRIT BLADES: FOR CUTTING EXTREMELY DIFFICULT MATERIALS NEW

Fig. 4-19. Saber saw blades.

the sharpening or damage to the teeth will occur. As a rule, most woodworkers do not sharpen reciprocating saw blades, but instead discard the dull blade and replace with a new one as needed. While this approach may quickly solve the problem of a dull blade, it is wasteful as these blades can be sharpened with just a little care. If you are in the habit of discarding used reciprocating saw blades, consider saving a few and try sharpening them at your leisure. Once you have successfully sharpened one blade you will be sorry you ever threw one away.

All reciprocating saw blades are sharpened in the same manner. First the blade is removed from the power tool and sandwiched between two pieces of hardwood so that the gullets between the teeth are just above the hardwood. Next, clamp this unit in a bench vise so that the blade and hardwood are on a horizontal plane. Using a suitable slim taper file, begin filing the tooth faces at about eight degrees right and left, or to the original shape and bevel of the teeth. As a guide, the teeth at the

Fig. 4-20. Sharpen saber saw blades with a file. Hold the blade between two pieces of scrap lumber in a bench vise.

back end of the blade (where it is fastened into the saw) rarely show any signs of wear and can be used as a guide. File all teeth carefully and in a few minutes you will have a perfectly sharp reciprocating saw blade (Fig. 4-20).

Bandsaw Blades

While the bandsaw is a rather specialized woodworking shop machine used in making cuts for furniture and cabinets, it can be found in many home workshops. The bandsaw is really a jigsaw with greater capabilities and much more versatility. Some of the more common uses for a bandsaw include making cuts in lumber up to six inches thick (an impossibility with any jigsaw), cutting perfect curves, intricately-shaped contours, and even scrollwork. There are a number of different cutting bands or blades for the typical bandsaw and some are easier to sharpen than others (Fig. 4-21).

I think it is safe to say that most owners of bandsaws do not spend the time to sharpen the dull band, but instead replace a dull blade with a new one when the need arises. While this is the easiest way to continued use, it is wasteful because a bandsaw blade can be sharpened with just a bit of care and time.

The first step in sharpening a bandsaw blade is to clamp the blade between two blocks of hardwood so that a section of it can be worked on without it moving. It is advisable to disconnect the bandsaw from the power source to eliminate the possibility of the motor turning on during the sharpening operation. Next, the teeth on the band must be set proportionate to the width of the blade and tooth depth. The set of the teeth must also be paral-

Fig. 4-21. A bandsaw is very handy in the woodworking shop (ShopSmith).

lel to the blade back and not angled. As a rule, more set promotes free cutting on curves, while less set gives better tracking for straight cuts. The most efficient way to set the teeth on a bandsaw is to use a special tooth setting tool which should be available from any large store that sells a variety of tools (Sears, for example). Set as many teeth as you possibly can with the blade in the clamped position, then remove the clamp and rotate the band, reclamp, and set more teeth. Continue this approach until all of the teeth on the band have been set.

The next step after setting all of the teeth is to file the teeth to restore a 90 degree chisel tip on each tooth. A slim taper triangular file is best for this task. Take care not to deepen the gullets by filing too much. You will notice that each of the teeth has a hook—alternating from left, then right, etc.—and this is produced by tilting the file to achieve this bevel. It is always best to use the same number of strokes with the file for each tooth. File all the teeth that set toward you first, then reverse the blade and file all of the other teeth using the same technique.

The last step in sharpening a bandsaw blade is to install the blade in the saw properly. Then, with the saw motor turned on, lightly touch an oilstone to each side of the running blade. This will equalize the tooth set for the entire blade and in general make it cut better. When doing this, work very carefully and keep in mind that the idea is to just *lightly* touch the oilstone to the moving blade.

SHAPING TOOLS

The well-equipped woodworking shop will contain a number of power tools designed for shaping lumber. The more common of these are the router, jointer, and molding-head cutter. While there are other tools that can be used for shaping, these remain the most popular and we will limit our sharpening discussion to them.

Router

According to a recent survey by a popular do-it-yourself magazine, the most popular hand-held electric tool in American home workshops is the router. This handy tool is almost indispensable for many different types of woodworking projects. Basically, a router consists of a high-speed electric motor capable of 25,000 rpm, a chuck for holding the cutting bit, and an adjustable base (Fig. 4-22).

There are basically two different sizes of routers available—one-handed and two handed versions. In addition, most radial arm saws have a special router chuck on the side of the power unit that can be used to hold router bits, thus adding versatility to the radial arm saw. There are many different types of cutting bits for routers, which accounts in part for the popularity of this tool (Fig. 4-22). Some cutting bits have pilot bearings for guiding the cutter around the edge of the work while others do not. The latter type of cutters require some type of guidance system—either clamped to the work or to the router housing itself—to keep the router in a predetermined position during the task being attempted.

As a rule, only steel router cutters can be sharpened in the home workshop. This rule, of course, eliminates the popular carbide-tipped router cutters which, when they finally become dull, must be sharpened by a professional sharpening device.

There are two design types of router cutters that can be sharpened by the do-it-yourselfer—single and double flute. As you may have guessed, the single flute bits are easier to sharpen because there is half as much whetting involved. Upon close inspection, you will note that the single fluted router cutter has a compound cutter angle. The flat cutter face has a black slope, but it also slants to the left. Double fluted router cutters are simply two cutting surfaces with a compond bevel as well.

To sharpen a router cutter (either single

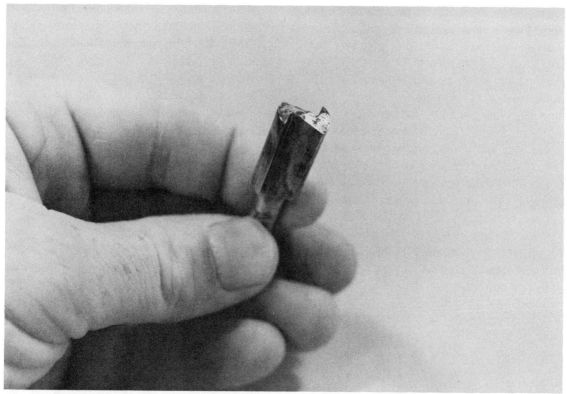

Fig. 4-22. Router bit.

or double fluted), begin by first removing the cutter from the router. Next inspect the cutter for any signs of damage. If damage is present you must first grind the end of the bit off square. A good approach for this is to chuck the bit in the router, then while it is spinning, slowly lower it against a flat carborundum stone. Next you must grind the steeper back sloping angle but do not remove the slot or land which is in the deepest recess of the cutter. The final step is to whet the land (or lands if a double fluted bit) to an angle of eight degrees. Work carefully to keep the bevel constant throughout its entire length (Fig. 4-23). As soon as the bevel reaches the edge of the cutter, consider the sharpening complete. The bit is ready for service.

If the router bit you are sharpening has not been damaged, a lot less work is involved. You must simply restore the original bevel to the cutting edge while at the same time touching up the compound bevel. This sharpening is most easily accomplished with a small hand slipstone or small benchstone.

Jointer

A jointer, or jointer/planer as this stationary power tool is often called, is very useful for most sophisticated woodworking projects. This is especially true for those projects where more than one board is joined to form a flat surface. Examples of this type of wood joining include tables, cabinets, and other furniture projects. A jointer enables you to smooth, plane, square, or bevel angle joint edges for a tight, flush fit. It is also possible to bevel or chamfer a decorative edge and plane certain size surface areas to help alleviate imperfections and irregularities in many different types of both hard and soft wood. It is generally agreed among serious woodworkers, both amateur and professional, that a jointer will enable you to accomplish a variety of woodworking tasks that would be nearly impossible with any one other woodworking tool.

Assuming that the knives of the jointer are not chipped, nicked, or otherwise damaged, it is entirely possible to sharpen them while they are still in the machine. First you must check to see that the knives (there are usually three) are properly set in the cutter head. Since each knife is adjustable, it is possible that one or more may be slightly out of alignment. Perfect alignment of jointer knives means that all edges are parallel to the table surface and all are exactly the same height. Before sharpening then, it is necessary to make any adjustments to the jointer knives.

After all jointer knives are aligned, lock the head of the cutter so that one knife edge bevel is parallel to the table surfaces. Once you have the knife in this position, place two

Fig. 4-23. Use a small stone to sharpen a router bit.

clamps on the drive belt, one on either side. This will prevent the head from turning while it is being sharpened. (You have already, of course, unplugged the jointer from the power source for safety.)

Jointer knives are sharpened with a suitably sized oilstone. To prevent damage to the table of the jointer, wrap two-thirds of the stone in paper, leaving only part of the stone exposed; about ¾ of an inch should suffice (Fig. 4-24). The next step is to stroke the knife with the oilstone until a fine wire edge turns up on the backside. Remove this wire with a few strokes to the backside of the knife and the cutter is ready for service. Repeat this technique for the other knives on the head until all are sharpened. It is important that all jointer knives be given the same amount of sharpening

Fig. 4-24. Wrap half of a benchstone in paper before using to sharpen jointer knives.

so it pays to count oilstone strokes and give the same number to each knife.

It is also possible to touch up the cutter knives of a jointer while the unit is running but *extreme* care must be exercised. Begin by clamping a stop block on the front table of the jointer about two inches back from the cutter opening and parallel to the cutter head. Now with a paper-wrapped oilstone on the rear table, slowly lower the table until the stone just comes in contact with the cutter knives. Next, slide the stone once across the table. The stone must lie flat and the forward edge must rest against the stop block on the front table. Stop the motor and inspect each of the jointer knives. Touching up the jointer knives is considered complete when a very thin, bright line is present along the entire length of each cutter. As a rule this secondary bevel should be less than 1/64 inch wide—any wider and the cutter knives must be reground.

Grinding jointer knives must be done to individual knives on a bench grinder. Adjust the tool rest to form a 36 degree bevel on the knives. It is important when grinding each knife to remember to work with a *light* touch. If you force the jointer knife into the grinding wheel, it will burn and be totally useless. Work carefully to develop the 36 degree bevel on each of the jointer knives.

After the jointer knives have been ground properly, you must next remove the wire edge along the backside with a benchstone. Then the knives are ready to be reinstalled in the jointer head. Double check that all knives are in perfect alignment before using the jointer.

Molding-Head Cutters

Molding-head cutters are rather spe-cialized woodworking blades that are used in a stationary saw, either table or radial arm saw. While there is nothing particularly difficult about sharpening these (most commonly in a set of three blades), it is important to remember that they start off and must remain exactly the same length to be efficient. In all cases, molding-head cutters have a single bevel that is flat rather than hollow ground.

Before it is possible to sharpen a molding-head cutter, you must make up some type of jig to hold the blades so that they may all be sharpened at the same time. This sharpening aid will not guarantee perfect symmetry during the sharpening process, but will certainly put the odds of success in your favor.

Molding-head cutters are most commonly ground to a new edge but the work can also be accomplished with a suitable file. As a rule, flat or straight blades are ground, and those with curved edges are touched up with a file. In either case the blades—suitably fastened in the jig—are filed or ground into the cutting teeth. Your intention, as with all sharpening, is to reestablish the original bevel as precisely as possible.

If you find that your molding-head cutter only needs a light sharpening, this work can be quickly accomplished with a small abrasive file or gouge slip. Another possibility for light sharpening is a hand-held abrasive wheel, such as those used for sharpening a chain saw. It is important to bear in mind, however, that you must choose a suitable size stone for the work (Fig. 4-25).

BORING TOOLS

Since so many projects around the home require a hole, the average home workshop should be well equipped in this area. Hand-held electric drills are one of the most popular tools in America and range in price from around $20 for a basic unit to over $200 for a professional grade tool. There are a number of features that can add to the price as well as the versatility of the tool (Fig. 4-26).

Because of the popularity of the hand-held electric drill, there is a vast assortment of attachments that can be used on almost any model. While we will limit ourselves to a discussion sharpening drill bits, I would like to mention in passing that the conventional drill can be used for almost anything from pumping out the basement to stirring paint. We will have to leave a discussion of these special attachments for another time and get on with the business of sharpening at this point.

The most popular drill bit in use today at the consumer level is the common twist drill (Fig. 4-27). These handy spiral shafts are simply chucked into the jaws of a drill and are used for making simple holes in almost any material. If special materials are being drilled, there are also special twist drill bits to help accomplish the task—a masonry bit for drilling holes in concrete, for example. Twist drill bits are not difficult to sharpen, and it should be mentioned

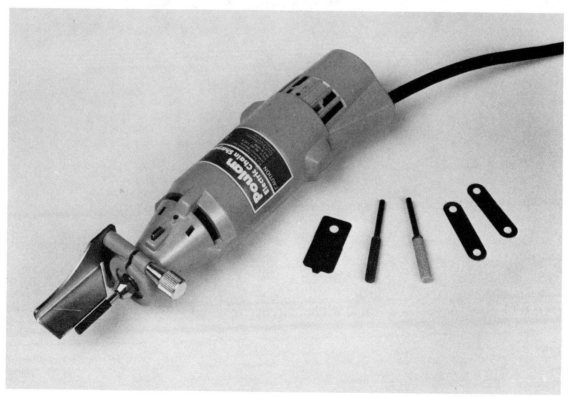

Fig. 4-25. Electric chain saw sharpening tool may be used on molding-head cutters.

Fig. 4-26. Electric drill.

that a number of special sharpening machines have come onto the market in recent years to greatly simplify the process.

In addition to the ever-popular twist drill, there are also a few other drill bits that are useful for special situations. Some that are worth mentioning are the spade drill bit, rim cutting bit, countersink bit, and hole or circle cutter. A brief discussion of each of these follows.

Spade drill bits are simply a shaft of steel with a flattened end—the spade—which is beveled so that it scrapes more than actually cuts as it passes through the work (Fig. 4-28).

Spade bits work fine as long as they are kept sharp; once they become dull they require more force to use and, as often as not, will not bore correctly. Spade bits are simple to sharpen as we will see later in this chapter.

Rim cutting drill bits make the smoothest and truest hole of all bits and for this reason are popular with woodworkers in the know. The bit itself has a thin steel rim with teeth that cut through the wood. Inside the rim of the bit are sharp, chisel-like cutters that peel away wood after it has been rim cut (Fig. 4-29). Rim cutting drill bits work best when sharp and worked at a relatively slow speed. These bits

Fig. 4-27. Twist drill bit.

Fig. 4-28. Spade drill bit.

actually have two cutting surfaces but can be sharpened in the home workshop.

The countersink drill bit is a rather specialized bit used in woodworking projects that will be fastened with wood screws. Countersink drill bits, as the name suggests, not only bore a hole for the wood screw but for the special countersunk head of the screw as well (Fig. 4-30). Thus one drill bit does the work of two. A variety of countersink drill bits are available and all can generally be sharpened at home.

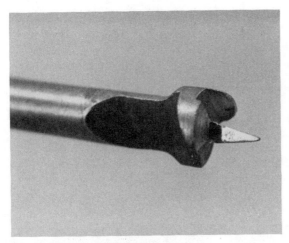

Fig. 4-29. Rim cutting drill bit.

One last drill bit that you might find around a home workshop is a special hole or circle cutter. While there are a number of different types of these, they all seem to have a twist drill center and some sort of adjustable cutter that spins and at the same time cuts a hole. Some of these can be sharpened by the do-it-yourselfer and others cannot even be sharpened by a professional sharpening shop. As a rule, if the circle cutter can be sharpened, the work can be done by anyone with a file or benchstone.

Twist Drill Bits

A twist drill has two cutting lips that are ground to the same length and at an angle of 59 degrees to the axis of the bit. The drill must have lip clearance, that is, the metal must be ground off just back of the cutting lips to allow them to contact the work. Make yourself a template from cardboard (or better yet sheet steel) and use it to help you develop this angle (Fig. 4-31).

A twist drill is sharpened by grinding either on the face or side of a bench grinder. First adjust the tool rest so that its surface is horizontal in relation to the wheel (Fig. 4-32). Next, scribe guidelines on the tool rest to indicate a 59 degree angle. Now when the drill bit is laid parallel to this guideline and laying flat on the tool rest, the tip of the drill will be ground to a perfect 59 degree angle.

The drill bit is ground by holding it securely at the 59 degree mark. Next, the cutting lip is held against the spinning grinding wheel and turned slightly to the right and slightly raised to obtain correct lip clearance. When turning, keep in mind that you do not want to turn so much that you come in contact with the other lip. By turning the drill bit slightly, the surface just back of the cutting lip is barely rounded. This is the compound angle you must achieve as it affords a stronger backing to the lips and will thus stay sharper longer.

As you grind, strive to keep the drill bit cool. This means working slowly, so that it can cool naturally. Under no circumstances should you dip a hot twist drill in water to cool as this will take all of the temper out of the steel and it will be useless.

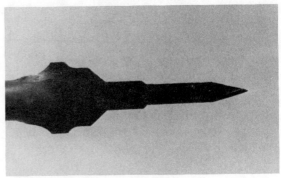

Fig. 4-30. Countersink drill bit.

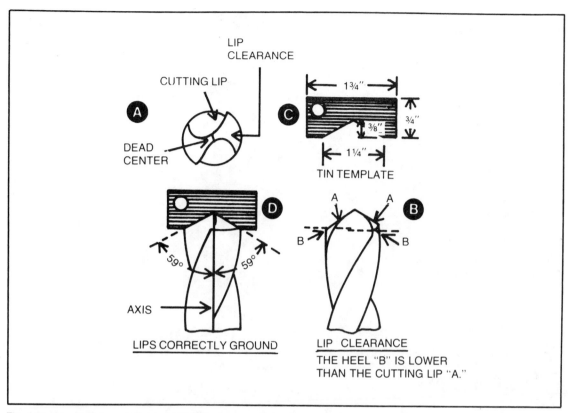

Fig. 4-31. Template for grinding twist drill bits.

Stop grinding often and check the angle with your template. Once you are satisfied with the bevel, chuck the bit into a drill and make a test hole in a piece of scrap metal. When a twist drill has a proper edge, each lip will cut a spiral coil of metal as it bores a hole (Fig. 4-33). As a rule, large holes in metal require a small hole—with a smaller drill bit—first. This makes drilling the larger hole easier.

Spade Drill Bits

Spade drill bits can be sharpened by two

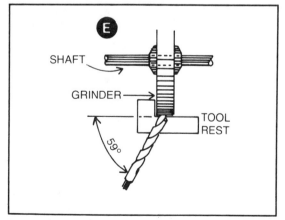

Fig. 4-32. Tool rest guide on grinding wheel for twist drill bits.

Fig. 4-33. When sharp, a twist drill will curl off equal amounts of metal.

methods: filing or grinding. A file is handy for quick touch-ups but a bench grinder should be used if the spade bit has been damaged.

To file a spade bit, first fasten it between the jaws of a bench vise with the cutting edges of the bit at a comfortable distance above the jaws. Some spade bits have one cutting edge while others may have two. In any case, the file is pushed into and over the cutting edge. If required—as in some of the larger spade bits—lift the back of the file gradually through each stroke to produce a slightly crowned surface on the topside of the bit. A few strokes of the file should be all that are required, unless of course there is a nick out of the cutting edge. If this is the case you must work longer with the file to restore its cutting edge.

If the spade bit has two cutting edges, sharpen one with the file before working on the other. Strive to maintain the original bevel and angle of the cutter. By filing into the cutting edge of the spade bit, you virtually eliminate the possibility of a wire edge forming on the cutting edge (Fig. 4-34). One other good reason for filing a spade bit (as opposed to grinding) is that the bit never gets too hot from the sharpening, and the original temper of the metal will remain intact.

Many prefer to sharpen spade bits on a bench grinder and this is certainly a fast and efficient way of accomplishing the task. Success, in this case, depends on adjusting the tool rest at an angle which will produce an 8 degree bevel on the cutting edge of the bit. It is also important to keep the shaft of the spade bit resting firmly on this base, while at the same

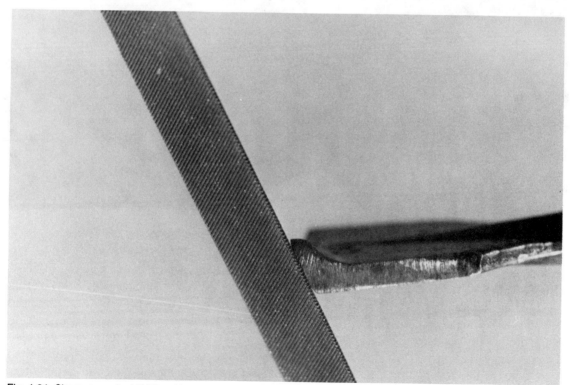

Fig. 4-34. Sharpen spade drill bits with a small file.

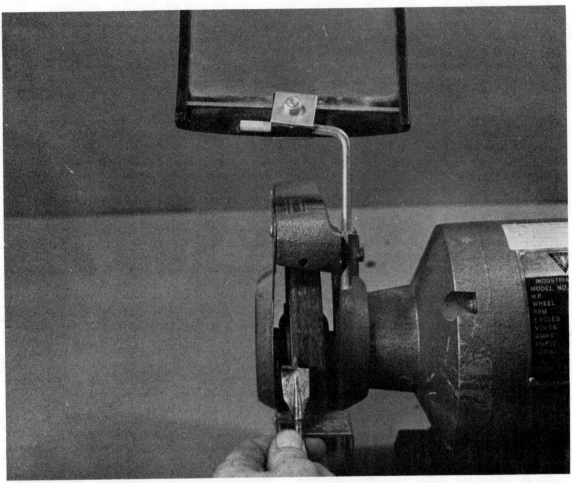

Fig. 4-35. Spade drill bits can be sharpened on a grinder.

time keeping the cutting surface which is being ground perpendicular to the spinning stone (Fig. 4-35).

Grind with a light touch when sharpening a spade bit. Do not attempt to remove too much of the metal, only enough to put on a keen edge. This assumes, of course, that no damage has been done to the cutting edge, in which case the cutting surface would have to be ground past the damage. Another good reason for not forcing the sharpening is that this would cause the metal to heat up unnecessarily. When this happens the metal will turn blue and the temper will surely be lost. Never cool a spade bit by dunking in water or oil as this will also destroy the temper. Instead, grind lightly, then stop work to let the bit air cool. After a few minutes grind again. Repeat this process until you are satisfied with the sharpening, then make a test cut.

Rim Cutting Bits

The rim cutting bits in popular use today will enable you to make a clean, crisp hole in almost any type of lumber, assuming of course that the bit being used is sharp. Actually, a rim cutting bit is sharpened in a manner which is similar to that used for sharpening an auger bit (described in the hand woodworking tool chapter). The main difference is that the rim cutting bit is easier to sharpen for it only has one cutting edge and a spur (the part of this bit that scribes the hole being bored).

I have found that the easiest way to sharpen a rim cutting bit is with a slim taper three-sided file. This should be done with the bit securely fastened in a bench vise at a height which is comfortable for filing. Begin by noting if any damage has been done to the cutting face of the bit. If this is the case, you must file the cutting edge past this point. If no damage has been done, simply file the cutting edge to a 25 degree bevel on one side of the cutter only as shown in Fig. 4-36.

After the cutting edge has been filed suitably, you should next turn your attention to the spur. This part of the bit is important from the standpoint of having a clean hole so it must be given a sharp inside edge. This can also be done with a file or, if you prefer, use a small stone. Often there will be metal burrs on the inside of this spur and they must obviously be removed during the sharpening. A few passes with a file or stone should be all that is required to sharpen an undamaged spur.

The last step in sharpening a rim cutting bit is to touch up the point of the bit. In most cases this is a three-sided point and should be filed so that all three sides are flat and crisp. Once again, a slim taper file is a good tool for the sharpening.

Countersink Drill Bits

Countersink drill bits seem to wear most

Fig. 4-36. Sharpen rim cutting drill bits with a file.

Fig. 4-37. Sharpen countersink drill bits on a stone.

at the point and this is where you should turn your attention. Unless some type of damage has been done to the bit, it can easily be sharpened with a small whetstone. After the cutting edges have been whetted, lay the bit on a flat surface and pass the stone over it several times while at the same time applying finger pressure so that the stone can cut true (Fig. 4-37). When working, keep in mind that the point must remain along the center axis of the countersink bit, or it will not drill holes that are true. Work carefully and in a few minutes you can restore a countersink bit to like-new sharpness.

Circle Cutters

A circle cutter, as used in an electric drill, actually consists of several parts. These include a pilot drill in the center—most commonly a twist drill bit—a beam, and the cutter itself. The position of the cutter relative to the pilot drill is adjustable by moving the cutter along the beam and, once in position, fastening securely. The cutter here is usually nothing more than a piece of steel stock with a beveled edge. In some cases the cutter can be reversed so that it cuts a bevel either inside or outside the circle. In any case, a circle cutter can be sharpened with either a whetstone or on a bench grinder. Probably the safest method from the standpoint of low heat is the whetstone.

When sharpening a circle cutter with a whetstone, you should strive to recreate the original bevel and this is not difficult at all. Simply use a circular motion while keeping the cutting face pressed flat against the stone. After the cutting face has been sufficiently sharpened, turn your attention to the flat sides and give them a few passes with the stone to make all corners sharp.

When sharpening a circle cutter on a bench grinder, you must first adjust the tool holder so that it will enable you to recreate the original bevel. In most cases this will be approximately 45 degrees. Any time you use a bench grinder for sharpening you run the risk of heating the tool beyond the temper point. If the cutter becomes hot, let it cool naturally in the air. Never attempt to cool the cutter by immersing it in water or oil to cool as this will cool it too quickly and cause the steel to lose its temper.

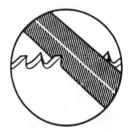

Chapter 5

Hand Garden Tools

American homeowners spend tremendous amounts of time and energy to keep their lawns, shrubbery, and flower beds looking good (Fig. 5-1). While some tasks—such as trimming the lawn and tilling the garden soil—are accomplished with the aid of power tools (lawn mower and tiller, for example), most landscaping and maintenance is done with muscle power and hand garden tools. Since most gardening tools have a cutting edge, they become dull with use and require more effort to operate or simply are not efficient.

Gardening tools are not unlike woodworking tools in that they are a big investment and one that you hope will provide good service for a long period of time. As a rule, you should buy the best gardening tools you can afford, for these will be made from good steel

and will generally be of sound construction which translates into a long and useful life. As you will see in this chapter, there are a number of things that can be done to extend both the life and usefulness of your gardening tools.

CARE OF GARDEN TOOLS

Before we get into the actual nuts and bolts of sharpening the various types of hand garden tools, let's spend some time talking about what can be done to extend the life of most tools. Two problems seem to plague most garden tools (in addition to being dull). These are rust and the deterioration of wooden handles.

Because garden tools are used outdoors and often left out in the weather during the summer months, rust can become a problem.

Fig. 5-1. The home gardener needs a few sharp tools to work effectively.

This insidious oxidation begins when the conditions are right—moisture, time, and bare metal. One of the prerequisites of a good garden is water, so it is probably safe to say that if you use tools in the garden they will get wet. As tools are used for digging, pruning, clipping, and raking they tend to wear slightly and thus expose themselves to the weather. As time moves on from planting to harvest, these bare metal surfaces which are exposed to moisture will rust. After a few seasons of this, the metal will lose much of its strength and finally break, crack, or otherwise be rendered useless. A shovel, for example, can become totally useless after just one season, if left out in the garden.

The best way to prevent rust on garden tools is to reduce the conditions that are conductive for the growth of rust. In short, keep metal surfaces covered, keep the tools dry, and store garden tools out of the weather whenever not in use. In addition, there are also a few things that can be done to garden tools if you should see some signs of rust appearing, such as keeping metal surfaces lubricated or in some cases painted. As I cover how to sharpen the various types of gardening tools I will point out how to protect metal surfaces.

Wooden handles of gardening tools will dry out in time; this is something you can depend on. When tools are new they are commonly varnished or painted to protect the wood, but as time goes on, the wood will expand and contract as a result of being exposed to the elements. A new shovel handle, for example, will be reduced to bare and dried out wood after just one season of use.

The best protection for wooden handles on garden tools is to store them out of the weather when not in use. (This is easier said than done.) Failing this, the next best thing you can do it to apply a coat of linseed oil to the wooden handles. This should be done as often as needed, but certainly at the beginning of the season and again before the tools are stored for the winter. It is also advisable to sand wooden handles with a medium or fine grit abrasive before applying the linseed oil. This small act will remove high spots on the handle and make the tool easier to work with. A dried out wooden handle on a shovel or rake is one of the best sources of splinters that I know of (Fig. 5-2).

Another effective means of protecting wooden garden tool handles is to paint them with a good exterior paint. Semi-gloss is a good choice. Not only will this serve to protect your tool handles from deterioration by the weather, but if you paint the handles a bright color, this will help you to spot tools that might otherwise be overlooked. A bright orange rake handle is much easier to see than a weathered wooden handle.

Some suggestions for success in painting your tool handles are in order at this time. First, don't paint your tool handles until after the first season. Give the original paint a

Fig. 5-2. Sand wooden garden tool handles, then apply a good coating of linseed oil to protect the wood from drying out.

chance to wear first. Secondly, before painting, sand all parts of the wooden handles to make them smooth and in a better condition to receive a paint coating. Next, plan on giving two coats of paint to the tool handles. The first should be thinned slightly with paint thinner or other suitable thinner so that it will soak in well. Apply the second coat after the first has dried hard. Lastly, do not think that because you have applied a paint finish to your garden tool handles that they are now indestructible. A long tool life still depends on storing your garden tools out of the weather when not in use. One last point worth mentioning is that you should check the condition of the paint coating often—every time you use the tool— and touch up areas that may have been damaged or when the paint starts to wear away (Fig. 5-3).

As long as we are on the subject of extending the life of home gardening tools, this

Fig. 5-3. Sand and paint wooden-handled garden tools.

might be a good time to briefly talk a bit about storage. It should already be very clear that tools should not be left lying around outside, but you should know that tools that are simply thrown in one corner of the garage will also suffer. The old saying "a place for everything and everything in its place" has some value when applied to the storage of home gardening tools. It constantly amazes me that people who take special pains to provide special storage for woodworking tools do not give the same treatment to garden tools. More often than not, garden tools are all stacked in a corner of the garage and it is truly an exercise in engineering just to get the rake out, for example. Is it any wonder that garden tools are left outside? The only obvious solution to this problem is to plan and construct a workable system for the storage of gardening tools. Let's consider a few things that may prove helpful.

A well planned storage system—whether it be for tools or supplies—begins with a careful determination of work and storage space. In some cases you may have a garage or carport that can be called upon to give up some space for storage of garden tools. If this is not your case, you should consider building some type of storage shed to take care of your storage (and probably workspace) needs. The popular how-to type magazines carry articles from time to time that may be of use to you in planning such a building. Another possibility, if you are less handy with hammer and nails, is to purchase some sort of storage shed. There are many types and seemingly in all price ranges. Some are made from aluminum while others are precut, kit-type wooden affairs. In any event, you should have some type of storage in or around the home.

Once you have determined the amount of available space you can spare for the storage of home garden tools, you must next take a careful look at the amount of equipment you need to store. The average homeowner will have most of the following garden tools: lawnmower, shovels, rakes, ax, grass clippers, hedge shears, hoses, sprinklers, wheelbarrow, and possibly some smaller hand tools such as a cultivator. The solution to the storage problem begins when you realize that some tools such as shovels and rakes are best stored hanging on the wall, rather than stacked in a corner. This means attaching some type of hanging tool storage rack—close to the ceiling—on your available wall space. You will find it easier to use a storage idea if it is simple, effective, and allows easy access to the tools being stored. There are currently a number of metal tool storage racks available; you should have little problem in finding some type of arrangement that will find your needs.

If you find that your hanging tool storage needs are greater than normal, consider building some type of pegboard rack for your tools. As an aid, take a look at Fig. 5-4, a diagram for a tool rack I have been using for many years.

In addition to long-handled hanging tools, you will probably have hand tools around the home garden as well. Little time savers such as

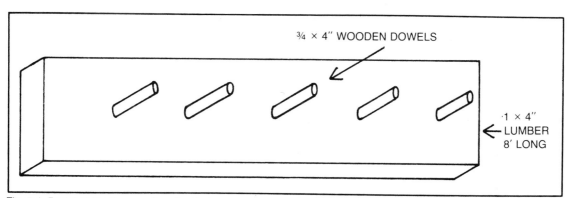

Fig. 5-4. Peg rack for storage of garden tools.

a hand cultivator or small shovel often end up in a pile somewhere in the workshop. Here again, you need to store these tools so they are out of the way yet accessible when needed. Some possibilities include: a pegboard with metal hooks such as those available from Masonite; a workbench with storage cabinets and draws; or a special footlocker-type storage box, located out in the garden.

AXE

It is probably safe to say that almost every American home has an axe, of one sort or another. There are actually quite a few different varieties of axes ranging from the simple one-handed hatchet to the two-fisted, double-bladed timber cruiser (Fig. 5-5).

Because of the nature of the work done with an axe, the cutting edge often suffers damage in the form of chips and nicks. Another common problem is breakage of the handle. Both of these problems can be solved with just a bit of work as you will see in this section.

Generally speaking, the design of the axe

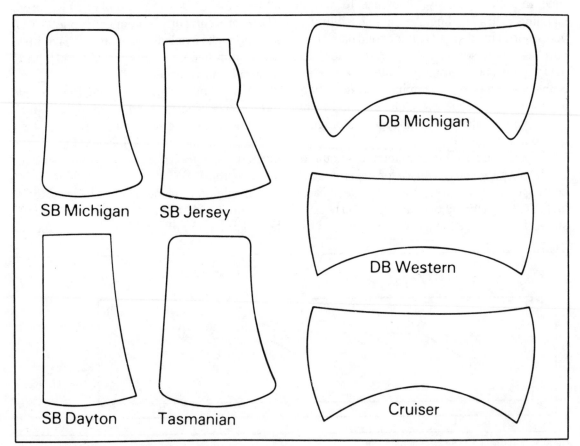

Fig. 5-5. The basic axe head designs.

head (and this applies to hatchets as well) will have a bearing on the type of cutting edge on the tool. A heavy duty axe, in the three to four pound head class, will most commonly have a cutting edge with a gradual bevel, while a lighter weight axe will have a cutting edge bevel that is very sharp, as in Fig. 5-6.

Your intention in sharpening any axe should be to duplicate the original bevel as this will be the best type of cutting edge for the tool in hand. The first step in sharpening an axe is to carefully inspect the cutting edge for nicks, chips, or other surface irregularities. If these are present they must be removed by grinding, then the proper bevel is started on the grinding wheel and finished with an oilstone. When grinding out nicks and chips, work carefully and do not press the axe head into the grinding wheel with too much force as this will cause the steel to heat up excessively; the end result could be uneven temper. As a rule, the steel should never become too hot to touch. Stop often to let the blade air cool. You must also keep the axe head moving constantly so flat spots do not develop along the cutting edge. Grind one side of the axe head first, then flip it

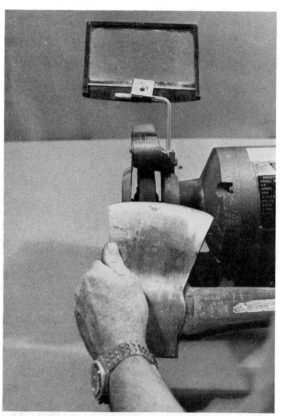

Fig. 5-7. An axe can be sharpened quickly on a bench grinder, but be careful of excess heat.

over and grind the other side. Continue this approach until the bevel on both sides of the head is approximately the correct angle (Fig. 5-7).

Because the temper of the axe head steel can be damaged by heat—a condition that is always present when working on a bench grinder—many people prefer to remove nicks and chips by other means. The bevel on an axe can be ground with a file, belt sander, or, if you are fortunate enough to have one, on a large water-cooled grindstone of the type that was common on farms years ago.

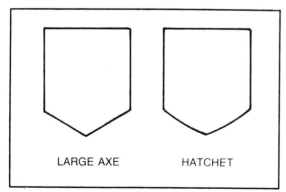

LARGE AXE   HATCHET

Fig. 5-6. Two axe head bevel designs.

A file is certainly a good choice for removing edge imperfections and irregularities on an axe. Since the chances of excess heat are almost eliminated, there is no danger of removing the temper from the steel. When working with a file, you should strive to duplicate the original bevel of the cutting edge. Clamping the axe in a bench vise will help the work progress smoothly. Long, smooth strokes will help you to work the steel efficiently. After the bevel is approximately duplicated, finish off the sharpening with an oilstone (Fig. 5-8).

A belt sander can also be used for grinding an axe without too much danger of destroying the temper of the steel. This method is not recommended if there has been extensive damage to the cutting edge, but it will work well for an axe in reasonably good condition. Begin by clamping or otherwise fastening your belt sander to a bench at good working height. Turn on the belt sander, which should have a 120 grit abrasive belt, and begin sharpening the blade with the belt moving away from the edge. It is important to rock the blade back and forth to produce a rounded bevel if required, or to hold the blade steady for a flat bevel. After you have the bevel ground, finish off the sharpening with an oilstone (Fig. 5-9).

After grinding the edge by any of the

Fig. 5-8. File an axe head to the proper bevel, then finish off the sharpening with a stone.

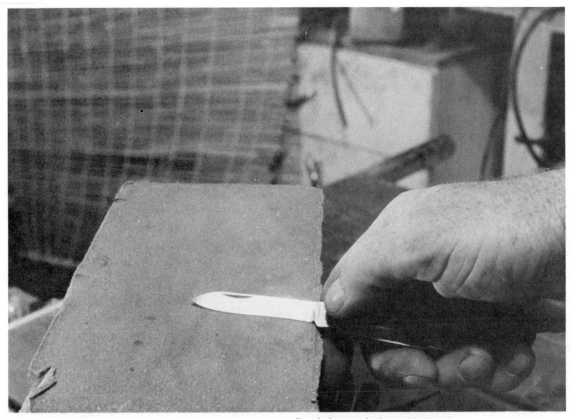

Fig. 5-9. A belt sander can be used to sharpen an axe, as well as knives and other edged tools.

methods described above, you must next use a stone to help produce a sharp, clean cutting edge. While there are specially-shaped stones which are designed for sharpening an axe, almost any good bench stone will do the job. Use plenty of oil or water during the sharpening. Use the stone in a circular motion, overlapping the circles as you work the full length of the cutting edge. The circles should run into the cutting edge rather than away from it. Work on one side of the edge first. Then, after it is fairly sharp, turn the blade over and give the same treatment to the other side. You can consider

the blade sharp enough when the axe can be used to whittle or shave in a manner similar to a pocketknife (Fig. 5-10).

In time, any good axe head will loosen from the handle and become dangerous to use—the potential for the head flying off will be greater. During sharpening you should check the fit of the axe head—it must be *tight*—and correct any problem before it becomes serious. There are a number of methods used to keep an axe head on a handle and I will pass these along to you. One sure way to tighten an axe head to a handle is to drive a

Fig. 5-10. Final sharpening of an axe should be done with a stone.

small metal wedge into the top of the handle. These wedges, commonly available in any hardware store, cause the wood in the axe head handle to expand and thus make the handle and axe head almost one piece.

Another method used for making a tight fit between axe head and handle is handy if you find that the head is just *slightly* loose. Simply soak the axe in a pail of water. An ordinary bucket with about one gallon of water is used for this and the axe is placed head down so that the head is submerged in the water. The wood will absorb some water and, in the process, swell to form a very tight fit (Fig. 5-11).

Unless your axe handle is of one-piece construction (handle and head made from one piece of steel), you will probably have to replace the wooden handle sooner or later. Since many find this a chore that often turns out

poorly, this may be a good time to mention a few points that guarantee success. The first part of replacing an axle handle is to remove the old wooden handle from inside the axe head. The best way to do this is to drill out the old handle. Clamp the axe head in a bench vise and work with an electric drill and suitable drill bit until most of the broken handle has been removed; you should be able to push out the remainder. *Never* put an axe head in a fire to burn out the old handle as this action will ruin the temper of the metal and render the axe head useless forever.

After the old handle has been removed, begin fitting the new handle into the hole in the center of the axe head. The new handle should fit very snugly into the hole and should also extend above the top of the head as well. This excess is trimmed off prior to installing

Fig. 5-11. Soak an axe head in a bucket of water and the wooden handle will swell slightly to make a tighter fit.

wedges. Work on the handle with a rasp or Surform tool until it fits through the head. Then, with a saw, trim off the excess handle and insert a wooden or metal wedge. It is common for new axe handles to be sold with wedges so make certain when you are purchasing a new handle to get the wedges as well. Pound the wedge into the top of the handle and force the wood out against the inside of the axe head. You will know that the head is tight when you can drive the wedge no further. Finish off the job by trimming off any excess wedge material and the axe should be ready for service. If you discover that the head is not perfectly tight, you can often remedy the problem by soaking the axe head in a bucket of water as illustrated in Fig. 5-11.

ADZE

If you have never worked with an *adze*

(sometimes spelled adz) you have truly missed an experience in woodworking. When round logs are squared on two or more sides for use in log construction, they are hewn with an adze. If you have ever had the experience of working with this tool, you will know the value of a sharp adze.

An adze at first glance looks very much like a very heavy duty hoe; it can in fact sometimes be used for chopping heavy roots beneath the surface. Upon closer inspection you will note that the cutting edge of an adze resembles a one-sided axe or hatchet blade, an indication of the origin of this tool. An adze is sharpened in a manner which is very similar to that described earlier for an axe.

The main differences between sharpening an axe and an adze are that the latter can be separated from the wooden handle easily and this fact makes sharpening a bit easier. An adze can be ground to a bevel edge with a bench grinder, file, or electric belt sander, with the latter two being the preferred choices from the standpoint of low heat. You will want to give a final edge to your adze with a good bench stone, however, as this tool is most effective when *very* sharp (Fig. 5-12).

When working with an adze, you may find it necessary to touch up the edge periodically to keep it cutting efficiently. This will become especially apparent when working on dried timber or on many of the hardwoods. Look for and avoid hitting old nails that may be in the timber as they will take a chip out of the cutting edge and create all kinds of extra work for you. Work with a developed rhythm and you will find an adze an enjoyable tool to use for hand-hewn beams and rafters.

Fig. 5-12. File the bevel on an adze, then finish with a bench stone.

CULTIVATOR

There are actually a few different types of cultivators designed for both one and two-handed use. In all cases, cultivators are three or four-pronged rakelike affairs that are used for breaking up soil crust, light weeding, and cultivating (Fig. 5-13). Some cultivators are lightweight and are best used for aerating the surface soil around growing plants and shrubbery. Heavier cultivators are used (and these are generally two-handed) much like a hoe or rake in the garden. The real value of these longer cultivators is that you are not required to get down on your hands and knees to work.

It may never have occurred to you that your cultivator needed to be sharpened! Most gardeners simply keep on using one until the handle or one or more of the tines break. The truth of matter is, however, that the cultivator you are presently using will work much better if it is sharpened.

The important thing to remember when sharpening a cultivator is that you do not want to remove too much of the metal from any one tine. These fingers, which are used for breaking up soil crust, must be strong enough to flex without bending or breaking. The original design of the tine is intended to be worked in this manner for a lifetime and therefore should not be changed by excessive grinding or file work. Of course, if one of the tines has been damaged or broken slightly, you must grind all of the others to this height (Fig. 5-14).

The tips of the tines on a cultivator should be pointed but not thin. Needle-like points would break off or wear quickly when used in the garden. Broad points are therefore much preferred. When sharpening undamaged cultivator tines, you can use either a bench grinder or a file. If the former is used, be careful that the metal does not heat up excessively as this will remove the temper of the metal and it will

Fig. 5-13. A hand cultivator is very handy around plants and bushes.

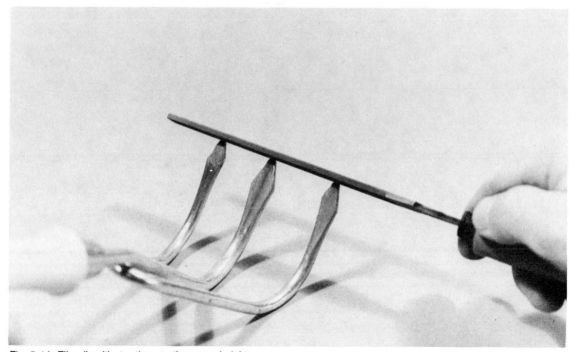

Fig. 5-14. File all cultivator tines to the same height.

probably bend easily; this would mean a totally useless gardening tool. If you use a file for the sharpening, clamp the cultivator in a bench vise to hold it securely while you work. The file, while not as fast as a bench grinder, poses little threat to the temper.

GRASS SNIPS

Grass snips are useful for trimming those sections of the lawn and garden that cannot be trimmed with the lawnmower (Fig. 5-15). Grass snips are, I am afraid, falling by the wayside as more modern gadgets such as electrically-powered Weed Eaters step in and take over. Personally, I feel that wandering around the lawn clipping long grass that the mower missed is a pleasant way to spend a few minutes. The electric trimmers on the other hand require much more energy to use—in *both* calories and kilowatts—and you are always connected by the electrical umbilical cord.

Hand-powered grass snips are easiest to sharpen if the blades can be taken apart and each sharpened separately. Unfortunately, this is not always possible as many types of grass snips have a riveted bolt where the blades are joined and on which they pivot. The sharpening is just slightly more difficult when the blades remain together. The trick is to use a smaller file to do the sharpening—4-inch mill bastard file, for example, or a small whetstone.

Fig. 5-15. Grass snips are useful for those spots the lawnmower missed.

There are some types of grass snips which are made from very hard steel. If you have this type, you will find it very difficult to sharpen them with a file. Your best bet in this case is either to use a grinding wheel or take the snips to a professional grinder. Since this type of sharpening takes only a few minutes on professional equipment, the charge should be minimal.

If you have the type of grass snips which can be sharpened with a file or stone, begin by opening them as far as they will go—if you can take the blades apart, you should do this—and then brace one of the blades against a solid work surface. Sharpen this supported blade first. Holding the file at an angle of about 80 degrees (or the original angle if it differs from this standard), file in smooth, even strokes. You can and should use the existing bevel as a guide for sharpening. Check the back edges of the blades, as these areas tend to wear less than the forward sections. The filing will be a bit easier if you start from the pivot point of the two blades and work your way toward the tips. Sharpen one blade at a time. When you are satisfied with the first one, turn the snips over and file the second blade (Fig. 5-16). It is not necessary to file off the wire edge which forms on the backside of the blades; simply closing the snips a few times will cause these to wear off.

Instead of using a file, you may prefer to

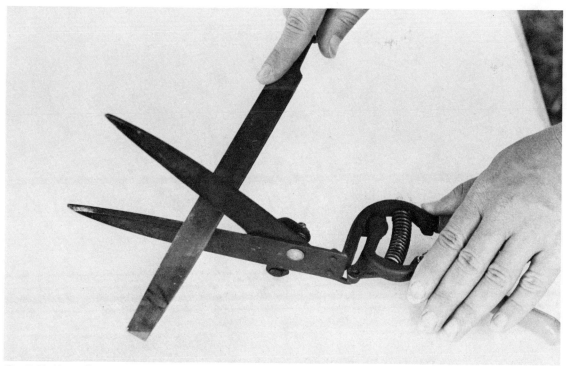

Fig. 5-16. Use a file to sharpen grass snips.

use a small whetstone. The technique is really the same in that you want to recreate the original bevel on the cutting edges. Work on one blade at a time and use a circular motion. You should apply a few drops of oil during the whetting. In truth, a bench stone will give a sharper cutting edge than a file.

After your grass snips have been sharpened to your satisfaction, you should next turn your attention to lubrication and general maintenance of the tool. Since grass snips are mechanical in that there are commonly several moving parts, you should check to see that any nuts are snug and that all moving parts move freely. In almost every case, closing the hand over the two handles causes the blades to come together in a conventional cutting manner. As the pressure is released, the blades should swing back to a fully opened position. In time all grass snips will become sluggish, requiring more effort on your part and in general being less efficient. Spot lubrication is usually all that is required to restore grass snips to first-class working order (Fig. 5-17).

HEDGE SHEARS

Hedge shears are another hand garden tool that is being replaced by an electrical version (the sharpening of which is covered in the next chapter). Hedge shears are a very effective way of cutting back and shaping hedges and ornamental shrubbery around the home

Fig. 5-17. Lubricate the pivot bolt and grass snips will be easier to use.

Fig. 5-18. Hedge shears are useful for trimming bushes.

(Fig. 5-18). With a little practice, you should be able to do a professional-looking job of landscaping without having to rely on electrical power. Success in trimming shrubbery is dependent on two factors: a sharp eye and sharp hedge shears. The former is developed over time and the latter is accomplished with conventional sharpening tools.

Hedge shears are sharpened in a manner which is very similar to the method used for sharpening grass snips except that the task is easier because the blades can be opened quite far. The most important point to keep in mind is that the new bevel should be very close to the old one—commonly about 60 degrees (Fig. 5-19). It is also important to keep a close eye on the bevel angle as it may change slightly from the rear to the front of the blade. It may be helpful to know that the bevel always slopes away from the inside blade toward the outer surface.

The tools which can be used for sharpening hedge shears are bench grinder, belt sander, file, or whetstone. Unless damage has occurred to one or both of the blades, you should use either a file or whetstone. While these sharpening tools are slower, they are safer to use in that the chances of excessive heat buildup are almost nonexistent; there is little danger of ruining the temper of the steel.

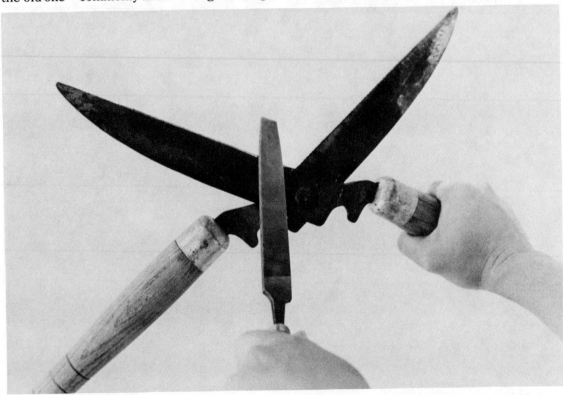

Fig. 5-19. Sharpen hedge shears with a file.

It is important not to remove more metal than necessary to develop a sharp cutting edge. Hedge shear blades are bowed and twisted slightly so that the cutting contact point moves toward the tip as they are closed during use. If excessive amounts of metal are removed, this contact point will be destroyed and the shears will never cut right again. Maintain the same edge bevel and sharpen only enough to do the job.

After sharpening hedge shears to your satisfaction, you should next turn your attention to lubrication and handle maintenance. As a rule, you should give a light coating of oil or silicone spray to all metal surfaces. In addition, you should also oil the pivot point so that operation will be efficient and smooth. Since most hedge shears have wooden handles, you should also give a little attention to these as well. As mentioned earlier, there are two ways of protecting wooden handles: apply a coat of linseed oil (or similar penetrating-type coating) or paint with a quality semi-gloss exterior coating.

HOE

Most home gardeners do not realize that a hoe will work much more efficiently if it is sharpened periodically. The need for sharpening a hoe is not always apparent since it is used at the end of a long handle—in effect, a lever—which masks its inefficiency. The truth is that a hoe should be sharpened to make it both easier to use and more effective at cutting weeds.

The best way to sharpen a hoe is with a file—a 10-inch mill bastard file works well. If the cutting edge of the hoe has suffered some damage such as an irregular edge or missing sections, you will find it necessary to use a bench grinder to make the edge true first, then finish off the bevel with a file.

Begin sharpening a hoe, if you are right handed, on the left side of the blade. In the ideal situation, first clamp the hoe in a bench vise at a convenient working height. This can also be done in the field by holding the hoe perpendicular to the ground, but this requires more effort on your part. Push the file downwards, from left to right, in one long and smooth stroke. It is important to hold the file at the same angle throughout the stroke to restore a consistent beveled cutting edge. The angle of the bevel can be from 45 to 85 degrees. The former bevel will cut fast but will not last as long as the latter. The most important thing to remember is that the angle being filed should be consistent along the entire edge of the hoe blade. In most cases, half a dozen strokes of the file will produce a good, sharp working edge on the hoe blade (Fig. 5-20).

After you have filed the bevel edge of the hoe you will, if you look closely, note a tiny wire-like metal edge along the opposite side of the hoe blade. You should remove this with a few light strokes of the file. Simply file flat along the inside of the hoe handle.

To make your garden hoe more versatile you can also sharpen the sides of the blade at right angles to the bottom cutting edge, as well as the normal cutting edge. A sharpened side on a hoe will enable you to pull small weeds out of the ground with much greater ease. Simply rotate the handle and use the side of the hoe for this work. The hoe that we have in our garden, for example, has a blade with an 85 degree beveled cutting edge and two sides which have been filed to about a 45 degree bevel. With this

Fig. 5-20. A file is useful for sharpening a hoe.

tool, most of the hoeing is done with the hoe held in the usual manner. But when a special weeding task is at hand, the hoe is turned on its side and the sharper edge is pressed into service.

After you have sharpened your hoe, spend a few minutes more to take care of the metal and wooden parts. First give a light coating of oil or silicone to the metal blade, connecting shaft, and metal ferrule. Then you can turn your attention to the wooden handle. Because it is a common practice to leave a hoe out in the garden, the wooden handle will dry out and become splintery in a short period of time. A rough, dried out wooden handle is one of the best sources of splinters known to man. Avoid the problem by first sanding the wooden handle

to remove all roughness, then apply a coating of linseed oil and let this soak into the handle. This type of treatment should last for several weeks of weathering. If you find that the wooden handle is still suffering from the elements, consider applying several coats of semi-gloss exterior paint.

LOPERS

Whenever medium duty pruning is called for in the home garden—most commonly fruit trees and shrubbery—the best tool for the job is a pair of lopers. While there are several different varieties, some of which develop compound leverage and some that do not, all have a cutting edge which is similar. The typical loper blade works against a hook or cutting bar which is square-edged and not sharpened. The cutting blade itself will have only one beveled edge; this may in some cases be a compound bevel. When sharpening, strive to duplicate the original bevel.

For a thorough sharpening job, you should take lopers apart so you can put a keen edge along the entire bevel. If the cutter has been damaged, you must first grind the metal to remove the damaged area, then work with a file to restore the original bevel. In most cases it is advisable to finish off the sharpening with a bench stone. Oil the stone first. Then, with a circular motion, hone the edge to knifelike sharpness (Fig. 5-21).

Fig. 5-21. File the bevel on lopers carefully.

After the cutting edge has been sharpened to your satisfaction, you should next turn your attention to the cutting hook or bar—the other half of the lopers. Both the hook and straight types of cutting bars should be square along leading edges (at an angle of 90 degrees to the blade). Time and heavy use will contribute to rounding off this edge and thus make the lopers cut less efficiently. Use a file to square off this bar. You will find a round, chain saw-type file handy for squaring off round hooks and a flat file for squaring off a rectangular cutting bar.

Once both the cutter and bar sides of the lopers have been sharpened and squared off in turn, reassemble the two handles and check the working action. If you find that the cutting action leaves something to be desired, consider installing a new bolt through the pivot point. This should eliminate any sloppiness and the lopers will cut through branches and brush as if they were new.

The last two things that need to be done to a pair of lopers during a sharpening and general reconditioning is to give all metal surfaces a light coating of oil and give some attention to wooden handles. A coating of linseed oil applied after a light sanding should make the wooden handles last longer and easier to work with as well.

MACHETE

For some gardening tasks such as removing light brush, no other tool seems to work as well as this import from the tropical climes. It is a fact that a machete will cut through fibrous material faster than any other hand-powered tool. It is lighter than an axe so it can be swung with authority. In many South American, Caribbean, African, and Asian countries, the machete is the main tool used for clearing land and harvesting crops such as bamboo and sugar cane. American gardeners in the know use the machete for similar reasons and, while not used as extensively, find it to be an indispensable brush-removing tool.

Although there may be differences in blade contour, shape, and thickness, all machetes are basically the same. The typical machete resembles a long knife with a blade that measures around twenty inches in length. The handle may be made from wood, plastic, or even bone and will be fastened to the blade with rivets or bolts.

A machete may be sharpened with any of the generally accepted sharpening methods described in this book—grinding wheel, belt sander, file, or oilstone. As a rule, the machete is not given a razor-sharp edge but it should be sharp enough to carve with. If the blade has been damaged so that chunks or chips have been removed, it must be ground beyond these surface imperfections. If the blade of the machete is not damaged, it should be sharpened with cooler working tools such as a file or bench stone. Excessive heat can ruin the temper in the steel and make it brittle, the end result being a blade that will chip easily.

When sharpening with a file, secure the machete in a bench vise at a comfortable working height. Determine the correct bevel of the cutting edge. Look toward the heel of the

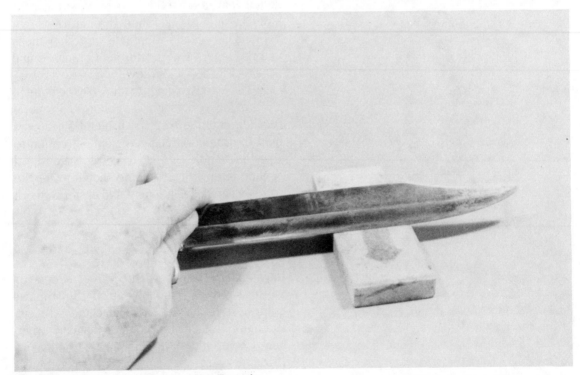

Fig. 5-22. Use a stone to sharpen machete-like tools.

blade, as this area commonly receives the least amount of wear, and duplicate this angle with long, careful strokes of the file. It is important to maintain the same degree of bevel along the entire length of the blade.

In most cases, when the blade of the machete has not been damaged you can sharpen this tool quickly with a bench stone. This can be done in the workshop or in the field, should the need arise. Hold the machete firmly and, using overlapping circular strokes, reestablish the original bevel to the cutting edge. Work from the heel toward the point of the blade, sharpening one side of the blade before flipping it over to work on the other side. Use oil or saliva for the whetting. A standard machete can be sharpened in this manner in a matter of minutes (Fig. 5-22).

After sharpening a machete, you should protect the metal surface with a light coating of oil or silicone spray. The handle of a machete should be tight. If this is not the case, peen over the handle rivets for a snug fit. When not in use store your machete either in a sheath or special carrying case (generally available from an Army surplus store) or in some other protective covering.

PICK

Whenever there is bull work type digging or trenching to be done around the home garden, chances are that a pick will be used for breaking up the soil. Used properly, a pick will not only help you to dig down deeply, it can also be used for breaking up and removing rocks, stumps, and other obstacles. Because of the nature of the work that a pick is commonly called upon to do, it is no wonder that this tool often suffers damage. In severe cases, repair-ing and restoring a pick is best left to a professional grinding service or blacksmith.

While there are differences in pick design, all picks have a pointed end and an opposite end which is broader. If this second end is *very* broad, the tool is properly called a *mattock*. Generally speaking, the pointed end of a pick should not come to a distinct point but rather be rounded to an area of about 3/16 inch. A "point" of this nature will not be damaged as easily as one which comes to a true point. If possible, the head of the pick should be removed from the handle and then ground on a bench grinder or belt sander. Since the steel of a typical pick is heavy, it will be difficult to heat it up enough to damage the temper. You should never allow it to get to the cherry-red heat stage, however, as this is usually in the range that will damage the temper of the steel. When grinding the point, remove only enough metal to develop the point properly and work as quickly as possible. Some prefer a four-sided point while others like a rounded point; I don't think that one is any better than the other. A square point is probably easier to develop on a grinding wheel, however, and therefore is the better choice.

After the point end of the pick has been restored, you can then turn your attention to the other end, which is often called the *main* end of a pick. This end is commonly ground to a 35 degree angled bevel on the bottom side of the tool. If damage has occurred to this area, it must be ground down until the area has been cleaned, then a new 35 degree bevel established. When working on the bench grinder, press the main end of the pick firmly into the spinning wheel but not to the point of slowing down the motor appreciably. This would cause the sharpening to take more time and would also be a source of excessive heat. Work carefully and establish the recommended bevel (Fig. 5-23).

After sharpening a pick, give the metal head a light coating of oil or silicone spray. Wipe the handle with linseed oil for protection, then reattach the head to handle. Store your pick out of the weather when not in use and it will last a lifetime.

ROSE PRUNERS

If there is one absolute fact about garden

Fig. 5-23. Grind the point on a pick.

and landscape, it is that shrubbery and bushes will take over if you don't prune them back. One of the handiest tools for cutting back foliage around the home is a pair of rose cutters. With one hand you can cut back all but the thickest stems and shoots. This tool is as handy in the orchard as it is in the rose garden and it will see many hours of use in just one season. To be effective, rose pruners should be sharpened at the beginning of the season and touched up periodically to keep them cutting efficiently.

Most rose cutters have one blade that, when the handles are pressed together, closes against a soft metal (usually brass) or plastic cutter bar. The typical design pivots on a bolt which can be removed for easier sharpening. There is also usually some type of spring which automatically reopens these cutters as you relax your grip.

The best way to sharpen rose cutters is with a small file or sharpening stone. Begin by disassembling the pruners and inspecting the knifelike edge on the cutter half. If the bevel cutting edge has been damaged it must be filed to remove the nicks or chips. While a bench grinder will make short work of this, it may also cause the blade to heat up excessively and ruin the temper of the steel. For this reason it is best to work with a file, using long, smooth strokes. After the damaged area has been removed, file a bevel that is the same as the original. Next, work with a stone to give the edge a final sharpening.

If the cutter edge of the rose pruners has not been damaged, or if you simply want to reestablish a sharp cutting edge, you will find a small pocket stone a handy sharpening aid. In most cases, a few lengthwise passes on each side of the cutter blade, maintaining the original bevel angle, will be all that are required to sharpen the cutter (Fig. 5-24).

After sharpening the cutter side of the rose cutters, inspect the condition of the cutter bar—the other half of the handles. Because this side is covered with soft metal or plastic, it has a tendency to wear or become misaligned. If this is the case, consider replacing the bar. Often a garden supply shop will sell such parts.

The next step is to reassemble the rose cutters. Make certain to replace any internal springs or other mechanisms that help to operate these pruners. The last step is to apply a light coating of oil or silicone spray to all metal surfaces (Fig. 5-25). You will also want to give moving parts some lubrication as this will aid efficient operation. When finished, the rose pruners should close easily and on an even plane on the cutting bar; once pressure is released, they should spring open quickly.

RAKE

A number of tasks around the home garden are easier to accomplish with the aid of a rake. Among them are breaking up spaded soil, finding and removing rocks, smoothing out

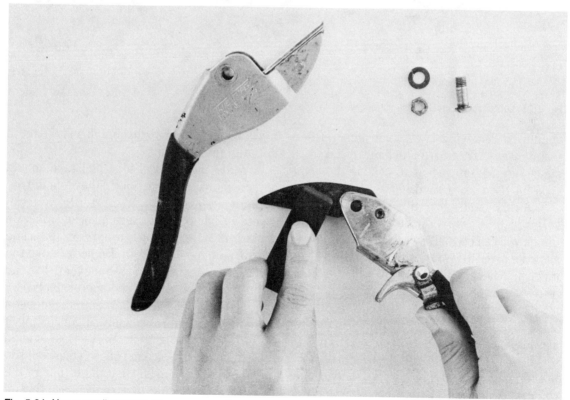

Fig. 5-24. Use a small stone to sharpen rose cutters.

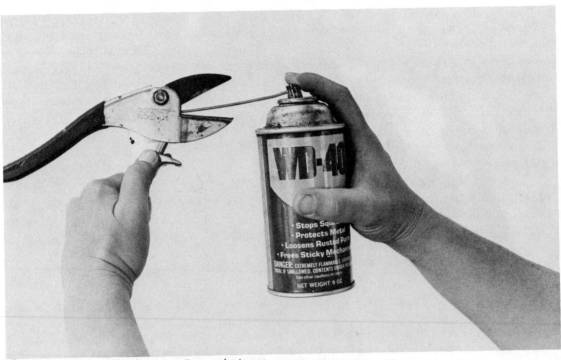

Fig. 5-25. Lubrication will make rose cutters easier to use.

seedbeds, renewing lawns, and general soil maintenance. There are a number of rake designs and it is important to choose the right type for the task at hand.

A rake is not generally sharpened in the true sense of the word, but there are a few things you can do in the workshop to the average rake to make it more efficient at the chores it is called upon to do. To begin with, the ends of the teeth on a rake must be all the same length. If one or more teeth have been damaged slightly, you can usually repair the damage by grinding all of the other teeth down to this new height (Fig. 5-26). If a tooth becomes broken significantly, you have only three choices: grind the tooth down and forget about it; weld on a new tooth; or buy another rake and

try to avoid conditions that break off rake teeth in the future.

While the teeth of a garden rake should not come to a *sharp* point, they should be pointed nevertheless. With a file you can create a slight point to the teeth of any rake. Be consistent in your work to develop the same type of point on each tooth. Do not remove too much metal, as this will cause the teeth to bend rather than rake when used aggressively.

After all of the rake teeth have been pointed, you should next apply a light coating of oil to the metal surfaces. As the rake is used this coating will be ground off, so you should do this on a regular basis. Give the handle of the rake a light sanding and apply a coating of linseed oil. This will help to keep the wood from drying out excessively and make the tool last longer. Some gardeners like to paint tool handles a bright color for protection, identification, and to make them more visible in the garden as well.

PRUNING SAW

A pruning saw is basically a crosscut saw that has been modified by the addition of an extra set of teeth which help in the cutting of green wood—which pruning obviously is. The teeth on a pruning saw are set alternately on opposite sides of the blade and they are also beveled on both edges of each tooth. This en-

ables the saw to cut in both directions and thus speeds up the work.

The pruning saw is sharpened in a manner that is not unlike the technique used for a carpenter's crosscut saw. Begin by clamping the saw between two strips of hardwood in a bench vise. Next, make sure that all teeth are the same height by running a flat file along the tips. All teeth must be the same height, so if any are short, all of the others must be filed down to this level. This process is called *jointing* and is discussed in detail in Chapter 5.

Begin sharpening with a 6-inch slim taper file (Fig. 5-27). File all of the teeth so that the

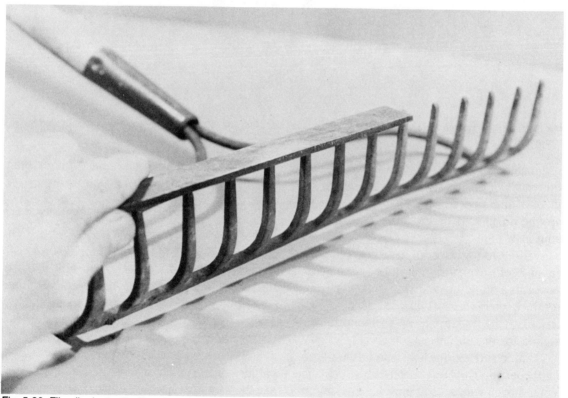

Fig. 5-26. File all rake teeth off at the same height.

Fig. 5-27. Pruning saw teeth are sharpened with a slim taper file. Clamp the blade between two pieces of scrap lumber, as shown here.

original bevel is reestablished. Most people find that working on all of the teeth that are set in one direction first, then turning the saw around to file all of the others, is the best approach.

After all of the teeth have been filed (the raker teeth are filed flat rather than with a bevel, as a rule), the next step is to set all of the teeth. Usually the best way to set the teeth of any saw is with the aid of a special tool designed for the purpose.

After setting, the saw should be given a light coat of oil and it is then ready for service. When not in use, store your pruning saw in a protective wrapper. You will add years to any saw by hanging it in a safe place rather than storing it flat.

SICKLE

A sickle is used for hacking down small strands of long grasses—or at least it used to be, until the electrically-powered versions came along. Now it seems that most sickles have found permanent places as wall decorations rather than out in the field. Nevertheless, a sickle is a very handy way to cut down patches of long grass around the garden and can also be used for knocking down rows of corn as well.

Sickles most commonly have a single bevel on the top side of the cutting edge. The best way to sharpen a sickle in the field is with a long-handled, oval scythestone. This stone is simply stroked along the cutting edge—from the handle, around the curved blade to the tip—several times to restore the cutting edge. If damage has occured to the sickle blade you must work with a grinder to remove the nick or chip. Often the best type of grinder for this type of work is an electric chain saw sharpener with the grinder guard removed. The small stone of these grinders enables you to work around the curved blade easily. It is important to maintain a smooth curve around the blade, so this will mean grinding equally along the entire blade. After grinding, reestablish the bevel, then finish off the sharpening with a long-handled stone.

SHOVELS

Since so much of the work around the home garden begins with a shovel, it is surprising that most gardeners give little or no attention to this digging tool. However, a shovel will be much easier to use if the cutting edge is free of damage and sharpened properly. While there are a few different styles and designs, all shovels are basically the same. This similarity spans all shovel designs from the long-handled digging shovel to the one-handed trowel. Some shovels are round along the cut-

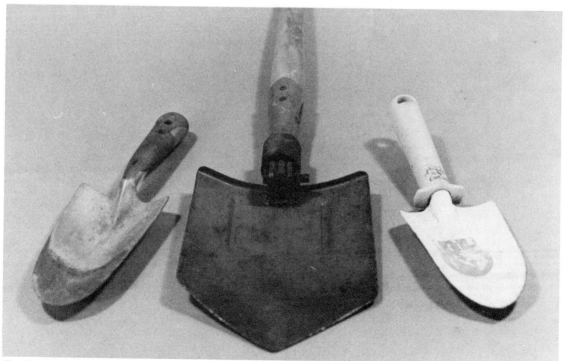

Fig. 5-28. Some of the many shovels used around the home garden.

ting edge, others may be slightly pointed, and some are even flat along the leading edge (Fig. 5-28).

A shovel (and other digging tools) will cut into soil much easier—even when brand new—if the blade has been given a few passes with a file. A standard ten inch mill bastard file works best for large shovels, while a six inch mill bastard file is more useful for smaller shovels. For standard sharpening where no damage is present along the cutting edge, simply file the inside of the shovel blade in smooth even strokes and at an angle of about 45 degrees, the common bevel for shovels. It is important for a good clean cutting edge to move the file in an even stroking motion around the shovel blade as you file. This will ensure an edge which is uniform. After a few passes with the file, a wire edge will form on the backside of the blade. It is not necessary to remove this wire because as soon as you begin digging, it will break off cleanly (Fig. 5-29).

When damage has occurred to the cutting edge of a shovel it must be removed before the shovel can be sharpened properly. Depending on the extent of the damage, you can use a file, belt sander, or bench grinder to clean up the cutting edge. It is important when cleaning up a

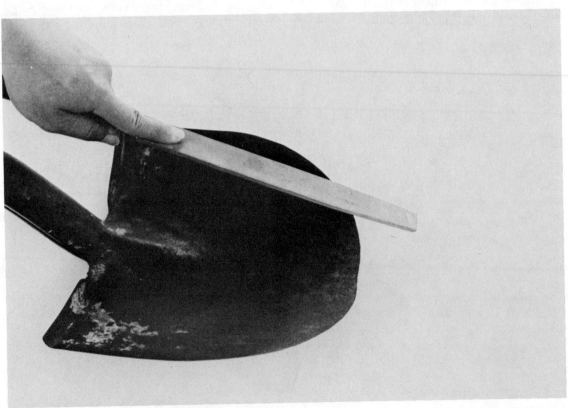

Fig. 5-29. Use a file to clean up the cutting edge of a shovel.

shovel blade that the blade of the shovel not be allowed to get too hot to touch as this would destroy the temper of the blade and result in a cutting edge that will chip or crack easily. You must also maintain the curve or straightness of the blade design and this is accomplished by constantly moving the shovel edge over the grinding wheel so flat spots do not develop. After grinding, file a 45 degree bevel on the inside of the shovel pan.

Once the shovel has been sharpened to your satisfaction, give the blade a light coating of oil, then turn your attention to the handle. If the handle has weathered, sand it to remove rough spots or these will be a source of blisters. Then apply a good coating of linseed oil. Instead of linseed oil, you may want to paint your shovel handle a bright color for identification as well as protection.

SPLITTING MAUL

The popularity of woodburning stoves has resulted in a vast selection of tools that are designed to make wood gathering, splitting, and storing easier to accomplish. One such tool is the *splitting maul* which, when used properly, makes splitting even the largest fire logs easy work. In reality, a splitting maul is similar to a conventional two-handed axe but with a much heavier head—six pounds is the standard.

A splitting maul has a cutting edge that helps the head pass quickly into and through the fibers of a log. To accomplish this, the cutting edge is rather blunt—commonly two 45 degree bevels—rather than gradual, as on an axe. The best way to sharpen a splitting maul is on a bench grinder; as long as you keep the tool head moving over the spinning grinding wheel,

there is little danger of excessive heat (Fig. 5-30).

After the two bevels have been ground on the cutting edge of the splitting maul, you should turn your attention to the head of the maul. Since this heavy tool (which is not unlike a sledge hammer) is often used for driving a

Fig. 5-30. Grind the bevel on a splitting wedge.

135

Fig. 5-31. The head of a splitting wedge should not be mushroomed.

pass along a few pointers on how to replace one. First, the old wooden handle is drilled out of the maul head. Next, a new wooden or fiberglass handle is fitted. Once the fit is snug, a special wedge is driven down through the top. Excess wood and wedge are then sawed off. To make the handle even tighter you can soak the maul head down in a bucket of water for several hours. This will cause the wooden fibers to swell and make for a very tight fit. (This won't work with fiberglass, of course.) Another way to secure the head is to give a liberal coat of fiberglass resin or epoxy to the top of the maul. Make sure the wedge and wooden handle absorb lots of the resin. They will expand and harden as a result of this treatment.

The last steps are to give the steel head a light coating of oil to prevent rust and to give some attention to the handle. Wooden handles tend to dry out and become splintery so the best way to protect them is to sand lightly, then apply a liberal coating of linseed oil. One alternative to this is to sand and paint the handle. This makes sense as the maul will then be much easier to spot in the woodlot, especially if it is painted a bright yellow or orange color.

splitting wedge, it will have a tendency to mushroom. These tiny pieces of bent-over steel can easily break off and become flying projectiles so they should be removed by grinding. The safest type of head on a splitting maul has rounded edges (Fig. 5-31).

If you use a splitting maul often, you will probably also break more handles than the average user. Since a splitting maul is useless without a handle, this may be a good time to

GRASS WHIP

A grass whip is very handy for knocking down large stands of long grasses in the garden. This tool (undoubtedly invented by a golfer) is swung in long strokes just above the surface of the ground and will make short work of clearing an area of long grass and even light brush. Basically there are two types of grass whips: those which have a blade that is part of the handle and those with a blade that is bolted

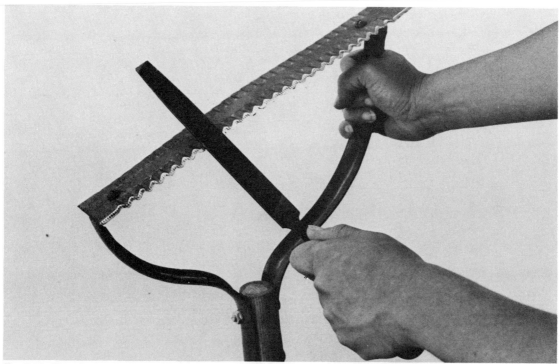
Fig. 5-32. Sharpen a grass whip with a file.

on to the handle. In either case the cutting edge can be restored quickly with a ten inch mill bastard file.

First determine if the bevel is on the top or the bottom of the blade. If the cutting edge is on the bottom, sharpening is simply a matter of holding the whip firmly—preferably in a bench vise—while sharpening. But if the cutting edge is on the top of the blade, you may want to remove the blade from the handle before sharpening.

Once you begin sharpening the blade of a grass whip, file at the angle of the original bevel. This is most commonly an angle of about 25 degrees. As with all sharpening, slow, even strokes will produce the most uniform and most desirable edge (Fig. 5-32).

After both edges have been filed, turn the blade over and remove the wire edge along the backside of the blade. A few light strokes with the file held flat against the underside of the blade should do this. If the grass whip blade is serrated you will not be able to remove all of the wire edges unless you use a round file (as used for sharpening a chain saw) in each of the serrations.

After the blade of the grass whip has been sharpened to your satisfaction, give the metal parts a light coating of oil to prevent rust. Then turn your attention to the wooden handle. Sand lightly to remove rough spots, then coat with linseed oil.

Chapter 6

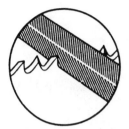

Power Lawn and Garden Tools

Most big projects around the home garden are accomplished with some type of power tool (Fig. 6-1). For example, in the spring when preparing the garden soil for seed beds and transplants, a power tiller will make short work of the project. During the entire growing season, in fact, the use of a tiller will save hours of manual labor as well. Mowing the lawn is still another task for which we must rely on some type of power equipment—the lawn mower. It is almost unthinkable to consider trimming a lawn, no matter the size, with shears or clippers.

For any piece of power gardening equipment to be of service, it must be both sharp and in good running condition. While maintenance of the two and four-cycle engine—the power sources for most gardening equipment—is really beyond the scope of this book, it may be

helpful to discuss some of the things that should be done to ensure that the equipment is operating properly. It is a fact that all of the sharpening in the world will be of little use to you if you cannot get the lawn mower started.

REGULAR MAINTENANCE

There are a number of things that can and should be done to your power lawn and garden equipment on a regular basis. Probably the most important and simple of these is lubrication of both external and internal parts. At the beginning of each season you should do the following before starting the engine:

☐ Drain the crankcase and refill with a quality oil of the type recommended by the manufacturer in the owner's manual (Fig. 6-2).

☐ Drain the fuel tank and carburetor and dispose of fuel in a safe place.

Fig. 6-1. Trimming the lawn is a favorite pastime in many parts of the country.

☐ Remove and clean or replace air filter (Fig. 6-3).

☐ Remove spark plug and squirt a few drops of light (10W) oil into the cylinder and pull the starter cord a few times to distribute this evenly. This will help to lubricate the cylinder and piston and reduce the friction during the initial start-up.

☐ Install a new, properly gapped spark plug of the type recommended by the manufacturer (Figs. 6-4, 6-5).

☐ Fill engine to indicated level with a good quality engine oil of the type and weight recommended by the manufacturer.

☐ Half fill the fuel tank with fresh fuel. If a leak in a fuel line or carburetor develops you will lose less fuel and have less fire hazard with this approach. If the engine is a two-cycle type

Fig. 6-2. Check oil before starting the mower and top up if required.

Fig. 6-3. A clogged air filter will prevent starting.

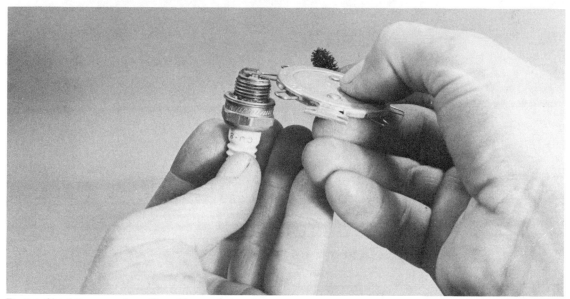

Fig. 6-4. Check the gap and condition of the spark plug often.

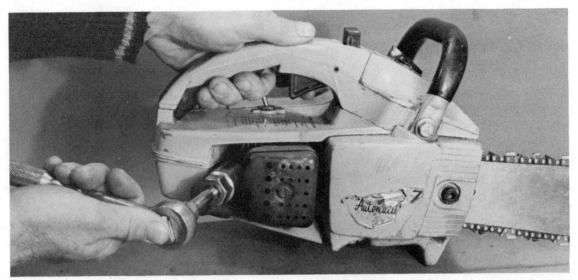

Fig. 6-5. Install a new spark plug as needed.

Fig. 6-6. Always use fresh fuel in the mower.

you must first mix fuel and oil according to instructions in the owner's manual before partially filling the tank (Fig. 6-6).

By giving your lawn and garden power equipment the kind of treatment briefly described above you will add years of trouble-free service to the life of the engine. During the season you should check the engine oil before you start it. Do this each and every time and you will reduce the chances of internal damage. An engine which is run without oil may sieze up in just a few minutes.

If you follow the instructions for care and maintenance that came with the piece of equipment, you will do it the most good. Change oil at recommended intervals and heed all cautions.

STORING POWER GARDEN TOOLS

There are a few things that should be done to your power equipment before retiring it for the winter months as well. After the gardening season is over, you should drain the fuel system and then start up the motor and let it run dry. Even though you have drained the system, some fuel will remain in the fuel lines and carburetor, certainly enough to run the engine for a few minutes. If this fuel is not taken out of the system in this manner it will dry out and leave a deposit which can easily clog the lines. Top off the oil reservoir before storing for a prolonged period of time. This will ensure that the bearings and other internal parts remain lubricated even though they are not in use. The last thing you should do to the engine is remove the spark plug and put a few drops of light oil into the cylinder. This will further guarantee that internal parts remain lubricated and reduce the chance of a internal metal breakdown.

Before putting the machine away you should clean all exterior surfaces. Sometimes, especially with lawnmowers and chippers or shredders, there will be a buildup of organic matter (grass clippings, etc.) and this material will encourage rust if not removed (Fig. 6-7). If you discover any bare metal surfaces you should touch these up with a matching paint to prevent rust.

Store your garden power tools in a safe area that is out of the weather. As an added precaution, you should also cover the machine to keep dust and other materials off of the exterior of the machine. Then in the spring, when you require the use of the equipment, follow those steps outlined earlier in this chapter for starting up. These easy-to-accomplish maintenance tasks will prevent a number of serious problems from developing and save you considerably in the long run.

ROTARY LAWN MOWER BLADES

According to industry statistics, the most popular piece of outdoor gardening equipment in use today is the rotary lawn mower. There are a number of accessories available—such as bagging attachments, mulchers, etc.—on these units which increase their versatility around the garden but probably the most attractive fact about the typical rotary mower is that it will trim the average lawn neatly and quickly. This assumes, of course, that the cutting blade of the mower is sharp.

Many gardeners do not realize that all rotary mower manufacturers recommend regular sharpening of the cutting blade, generally after every second or third cutting. Many home gardeners are quite surprised to learn that a rotary mower blade requires such frequent

Fig. 6-7. Clean the underside of the mower several times a season.

sharpening but once you understand how the blade works, you begin to understand the need for this attention. The need for regular sharpening of a rotary mower is often masked by the fact that the mower *seems* to cut. After all, all that is required is to start the machine and let it do the cutting. A careful inspection of the cutting that has just been done, however, is likely to reveal strands of grass that have not been cut. When you discover uncut grass after mowing, this should be your first clue that the blade needs attention.

While it is sensible to remove the blade from a rotary mower every so often, especially if it has been damaged by hitting a rock or other obstacle, you can dress up the blade while it is still on the machine (Fig. 6-8). This is the type of sharpening that should be done on a regular basis—say, after every second cutting. This sharpening can be quickly accomplished with a small file but there are a few things which should be done first.

Since it is necessary to turn a rotary mower on its side to sharpen the blade, you should first run the fuel tank dry, or, if the tank is full, empty the fuel into a suitable container. Next, disconnect and remove the spark plug. This will give you the opportunity to inspect

Fig. 6-8. The blade of a rotary mower can be sharpened while still on the mower.

the plug for signs of fouling or damage, in which case you clean or replace as required. More importantly, removing the spark plug eliminates the possibility of the motor starting while you are sharpening the blade. There are a few horror stories about rotary mowers starting as a result of simply turning the blade 180 degrees. Another practical reason for removing the spark plug is that there will be no compression in the cylinder and this will make turning the blade very easy. If your rotary mower has an oil bath air cleaner, this should also be removed to prevent spilling the oil in this filter (Fig. 6-7).

After all of the precautions listed above have been accomplished, turn your rotary mower on its side and carefully inspect the blade. If any damage is present the blade must be removed and taken to the bench grinder for grinding. If cracks are present, however, the blade should be discarded. A cracked blade has the potential to fly apart at any time and is therefore not worth trying to salvage. As a rule, small nicks can be ground out of the blade, but this means removing the blade first.

To touch up a rotary blade, begin by turning the blade to a comfortable working position. Then (assuming you are right handed) hold the far end of the blade with your left hand while you file the close end with your right. Since the bevel on the blade is on the topside, you must work the file between the blade and the housing of the mower. You will find it necessary to use either a short file or one specially designed for this type of sharpening. A blade sharpening file should be available at any lawn and garden supply center.

File with enough pressure to dress the blade in as few strokes as possible. At the same time, slide the file along the bevel so that it is filed evenly. Count the number of strokes required to give a keen edge, then turn the blade 180 degrees and give the same treatment to the other end. It is important to file equally on both ends of the blade to maintain balance. A blade which is heavier on one end can damage the mainshaft bearings in no time at all.

This filing procedure is all that is necessary to sharpen a rotary mower blade. You should plan however to remove the blade from the mower after every three to five sharpenings—or if damage has occurred—and check both the bevel angle and balance.

Removal of a rotary mower blade is generally a simple operation. Begin by completing all of the safety procedures outlined above—

Fig. 6-9. Remove the blade with a wrench.

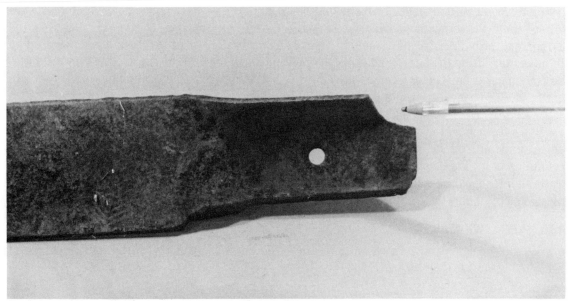

Fig. 6-10. A broken or chipped rotary blade spells trouble. Throw it out.

remove spark plug, drain fuel system, etc. Next, with a suitable wrench remove the center bolt which holds the blade in place. If necessary, use a block of wood to keep the blade from turning while removing the bolt (Fig. 6-9).

Once the blade has been removed from the mower, inspect it carefully in good light. Look for any signs of cracking, nicks, or missing sections. As a rule, nicks can be ground but cracks or missing sections indicate that a new blade is required (Fig. 6-10).

Inspect the bevel on the blade and if it is missing, regrind the edge to thirty degrees. Do this on both ends of the blade. Next, you will want to check the balance of the blade and correct if necessary.

To check the balance of a rotary blade, it must be suspended on a string and allowed to hang for a few minutes so that if one end is heavier, it will hang lower than the lighter end. Begin by passing the end of a rope through the center hole in the blade and tying a large knot. Next, hang the rope so that the blade rests on the knot. Watch what happens. A perfectly-balanced rotary mower blade will come to rest on a horizontal plane and this is what you are

Fig. 6-11. Hang balancing a rotary blade.

trying to achieve. An unbalanced blade, on the other hand, will hang with the heavy end down. To correct the problem of imbalance, you must remove metal from the heavy end. This should be done on a bench grinder in moderate stages until the blade hangs horizontally (Fig. 6-11).

Once the rotary blade has been balanced, and the proper bevel ground onto the cutting edge, reinstall it on the mower and secure the retaining bolt. The blade is now ready for mowing but should be touched up often with a file as outlined earlier.

REEL-TYPE LAWN MOWER

Reel-type lawn mowers were once the only type of lawn mower available and were extensively used by gardeners all across the country. The first versions were powered by muscle; later versions used a two or three-horsepower gasoline engine. Both types are basically the same and are sharpened in a similar manner (Fig. 6-12).

Reel-type lawn mowers cut as a result of the blades passing over a cutter bar on the bottom of the mower. Often, adjusting this cutter bar or plate will greatly improve the cutting of the mower. The cutter plate, because of its location on the bottom of the mower, is easily knocked out of alignment. When this happens the cutting efficiency of the mower drops off

Fig. 6-12. Reel lawn mowers are less popular than rotary types but there are still many in use today.

Fig. 6-13. Adjust the cutter plate with a screwdriver.

dramatically. As a rule, the cutter reel blades should just barely scrape the cutter plate as they revolve, so adjust the plate accordingly (the reel blades remain in a constant position and cannot be adjusted). Adjustments to the cutter plate are made with four screws, two on each side of the plate (Fig. 6-13).

The cutter plate can be sharpened easily with a stone or file (Fig. 6-14). Simply touch up the bevel on the front of this plate. You can do this on the mower or remove it and do the work with the plate held securely in a bench vise. After sharpening, readjust the cutter plate so that the cutter reel blades just miss it in pass-

ing. The thickness of a sheet of paper is often suggested as the proper spacing between the bar and reel.

Sharpening the reel blades on a reel-type mower is very difficult because the bevel angle on the cutting edges changes constantly along its length. Nevertheless, this can be accomplished with the reel attached to the mower.

The easiest way to sharpen the blades of a reel-type lawn mower is to use valve grinding compound, available at any automobile parts store. Begin by making a paste of valve grinding compound and water to about the consistency of peanut butter. Spread this along the cutter plate of the mower and then turn the reel backwards for a few minutes (Fig. 6-15). It is necessary to adjust the cutter plate properly before this sharpening and then again after the blades have been honed. Work carefully, wearing gloves to prevent cutting your hands. After a few minutes of backward turning of the reel, remove all of the valve grinding compound. Most types are water soluble and should come off easily with a strong stream from a garden hose. This procedure is the best—and probably the only—means of sharpening a reel-type lawn mower.

GARDEN TILLER

If ever there were a power tool that was developed to save hundreds of hours of back-breaking work, it would have to be the garden tiller. The very nature of the work a tiller is called upon to do is punishing beyond belief to tines of the machine and it will therefore be to your advantage to know how to keep them in good condition.

As a rule, the tines on a tiller are not sharpened in the true sense of the word, but they will cut through soil easier if they are maintained properly. Before working on the tines of a tiller, it makes sense from a safety standpoint to disconnect and remove the spark plug. This will prevent the possibility of the machine coming to life as you work on it. Next, carefully inspect each of the tines on the machine. Since most of these tines can usually be removed quite easily—a matter of removing a retaining nut on either side of the machine—you should do this first. Uniformity is the key to efficient tiller tines so your inspection should look to uncover chips or missing sections. If these are found, they must be ground off on a good bench grinder. Work carefully and remove only enough metal to make the edges uniform, at the same time not allowing the metal to heat up excessively as this will destroy the temper in the steel. Once the tines have been dressed in this manner, reinstall them on the machine and it is ready for service.

ELECTRIC HEDGE CLIPPERS

Electric hedge clippers make short work of trimming shrubbery and ornamental bushes but the cutter bar must be sharp to work efficiently. Electric hedge clippers trim leaves and twigs between the beveled teeth on a reciprocating blade and openings—or square-edged teeth—on a stationary comb-type bar. As a rule, only the beveled teeth on the reciprocating blade are sharpened.

Before the cutter bar on electric hedge clippers can be sharpened, this bar should be removed from the machine. In most cases this is a simple matter of disassembly. If you have never done this before, lay the parts out in an orderly fashion as you remove them so reassembly will go smoothly.

Clamp the cutter bar in a bench vise at a suitable height and, with a 6-inch slim taper file, sharpen the bevels on each tooth. Push the file smoothly during this sharpening, being careful not to take off more metal than is required to reestablish a clean bevel. Work on all of the bevels pointing in one direction first, then turn the cutter bar around and file all of the other teeth. Finally, run the file along the backside of the cutter blade to remove the fine

Fig. 6-14. Sharpen the cutter bar with a stone.

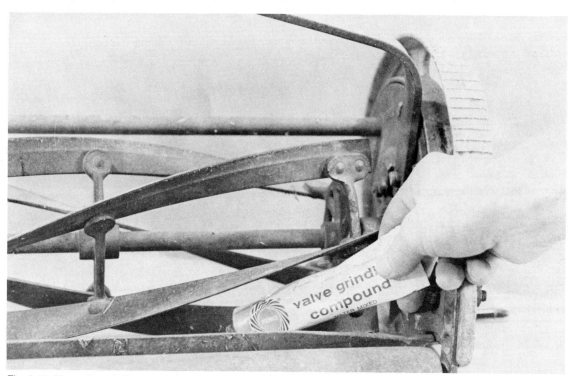

Fig. 6-15. Use valve grinding compound for sharpening the blades of a reel mower.

wire edges that will have formed.

The teeth of a hedge clipper can also be sharpened with a suitably sized bench stone, and many gardeners feel that this approach results in a keener cutting edge. The approach is the same, in any case.

After the cutter bar has been sharpened to your satisfaction, give it a light coating of oil or silicone spray and reassemble the tool. A few test cuts with the freshly sharpened clipper should reveal that the sharpening was worth the effort.

Chapter 7

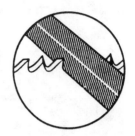

Chain Saws

One way the average homeowner can reduce the cost of heating a home is to supplement conventional heating with heat generated by burning wood (Figs. 7-1 through 7-3). In some cases, it is also possible to heat solely with wood and thereby realize a considerable annual savings in home heating costs. What is not generally pointed out, however, are some other related facts which I would now like to mention in passing.

Before realizing any type of savings in home heating costs, a few rather important factors must be present. You must have a woodburning stove which is hooked up in a safe manner inside your home and the unit must be efficient at burning wood. You must also have an inexpensive (ideally *free*) source of wood to burn in your woodburning stove. You must have the time and means to find, cut, haul, and

season your firewood. A pickup truck will help you gather and transport firewood easily, while a small automobile may make wood gathering an ongoing project. To cut firewood most efficiently you will need a good chain saw. This is no problem in this day and age, as modern chain saws are lightweight, very efficient, and relatively safe to operate. Few people ever have a problem with their chain saw in the first year or two of operation, but after this time period, it will surely require some type of maintenance and this will obviously add to your overall wood gathering costs.

One other fact of chain saw use is that the saw chain will not stay sharp forever. After the first few logs are cut up into stove-size pieces, the saw will start to become dull and less efficient at its task. This of course results in a greater time required for gathering firewood

Fig. 7-1. The modern chain saw makes wood gathering very easy (McCulloch).

and—if you place any dollar value on your time—greater firewood costs. If you want to keep your home heating costs at the absolute minimum, you should keep your saw chain as sharp as a razor (Figs. 7-4, 7-5). Most weekend woodcutters do not and probably the main reason for this is that they do not know how to keep a saw chain sharp. More often than not, the average woodcutter will continue cutting firewood until he or she is exhausted from trying to muscle a dull chain saw through logs. Then the chain will be taken off and brought to a professional sharpener. At present it costs about $6 to sharpen a 16 to 18 inch saw chain.

Fig. 7-2. The Dremel chain saw sharpening tool operates from a twelve volt battery (Dremel).

Fig. 7-3. Wood gathering has turned into a family project in many parts of the country.

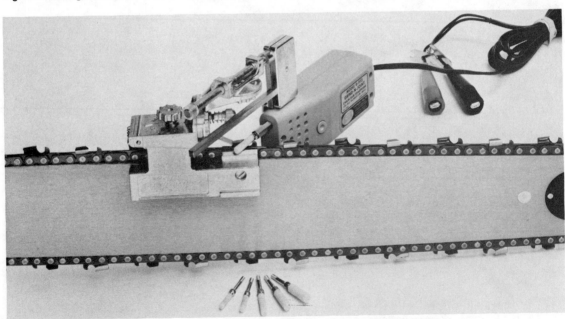

Fig. 7-4. Professional sharpening results are possible with the sharpening aids available today.

When you consider that a chain will probably require sharpening four to eight times a season, this can easily add up to increase your overall heating costs (Fig. 7-4).

Unfortunately, most people I have met who heat with wood (or at least supplement conventional heating with firewood), place little value on their time spent cutting wood or on the cost of maintaining wood cutting equipment. The general reasoning seems to be that cutting firewood is a good excuse for getting some exercise in the great outdoors with the added benefit of directly aiding in heating the home during the cooler months of the year. This is all well and good but there is one last thing to consider about chain saw use: A dull chain saw, in addition to being inefficient, is also *dangerous* to use. For safety's sake, it behooves the average do-it-yourself woodcut-

ter to learn how to keep a saw chain sharp. It is my intention in this chapter to explain how to keep your saw chain sharp. Along the way we will also look at saw chains in some depth so that you will be better able to judge the condition of your own saw chain. In the end, no matter what your reasons for cutting firewood you will be able to approach the task with a greater basis of information about the main tool used for cutting firewood.

SAW CHAINS

Most saw chains are composed of a series of *cutter links* (both left and right facing) and *drive links* (often called *center links*). All of these metal parts are riveted together to form a continuous flexible loop which is rotated around the bar by a special sprocket that is turned by the power unit of the saw (Fig. 7-6).

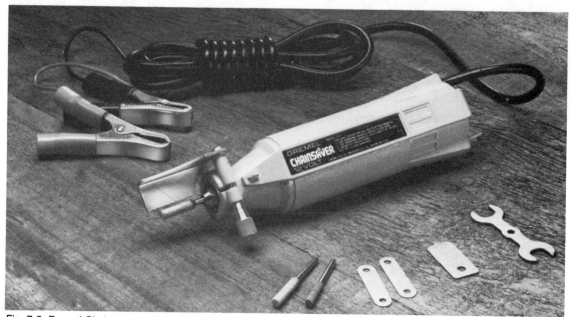

Fig. 7-5. Dremel Chainsaver is handy for sharpening in the field (Dremel).

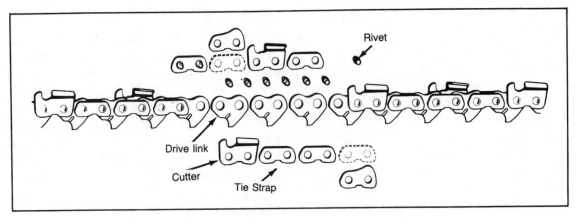

Fig. 7-6. Saw chain anatomy.

The main difference between any two saw chains lies, of course, in the design of the cutters of the chain.

Each cutter has a top plate which—if it is sharp—does the actual cutting of the log, and a side plate which spits wood chips out to the side, left or right. In addition, the depth gauge on the forward edge of each cutter determines how deep the top plate cutter penetrates into the wood each time it cuts a chip. Figure 7-7 clearly shows all of these important saw chain parts.

The most important parts of any saw chain are the cutters, at least from the standpoint of cutting ability and efficiency. At present there are four different types of saw chain cutters available. These are the *round* or *chipper*, *chisel* or *square-shaped*, *semi-square*, and the *automatic-sharp* type cutter.

The round or chipper type cutter (Fig.

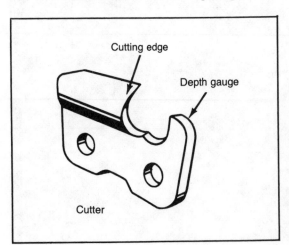

Fig. 7-7. Closeup of a saw chain tooth.

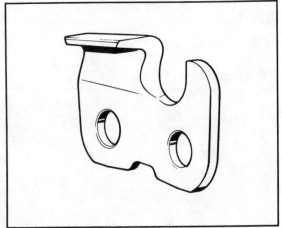

Fig. 7-8. Chipper tooth.

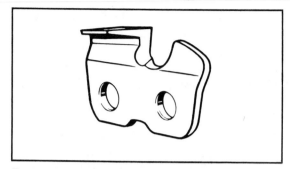

Fig. 7-9. Square tooth cutter.

7-8) is probably the most popular type saw chain cutter around, at least on nonprofessional saw chains. The chipper chain is the type of chain you will find as standard equipment on most chain saws sold today. It is easy to sharpen with a round file and some type of file guidance device. Chipper saw chains do not cut as fast as other designs but they are safer than other saw chains for the casual user.

The chisel or square-shaped cutter design (Figs. 7-9, 7-10) is fast cutting and for this reason is the choice of professional woodcut-

ters. This chain is easy to identify, as each cutter tooth will have a square edge rather than a round cutting edge. Chisel saw chains require more effort to sharpen properly; a special flat file with beveled edges is needed for touching up each tooth as well as a round file for cleaning out the gullets. There has been a new chisel type cutter introduced that can be sharpened with a round file, but it does not cut as quickly as the conventional square-edged chipper chain.

The semi-square shaped cutter design (Fig. 7-11) is somewhat a compromise between the round and square saw chain designs previously discussed. This chain can be sharpened with a round file and is therefore relatively easy to maintain. The semi-square saw chain cuts faster than the standard round cutter design, but somewhat slower than the classic square or chipper design (Fig. 7-11).

The last type of cutter design is found on chain saws that have an automatic sharpening device attached to the chain guard housing of

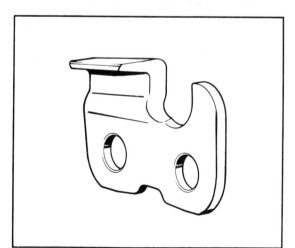

Fig. 7-10. Chisel tooth.

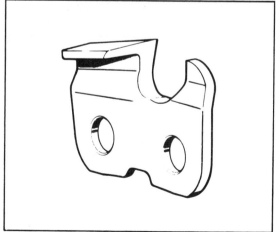

Fig. 7-11. Semi-square cutter tooth.

the saw. This is a full chisel cutter design that is distinctive looking in that each cutter faces upward (Fig. 7-12). This special positioning of the cutters puts them in alignment with a sharpening device that effectively "touches-up" each cutter when the sharpener is lowered into position. The sharpening device itself is a clever design which utilizes a man-made abrasive sharpening stone for the actual sharpening. Generally speaking, the self-sharpening chain saw design virtually eliminates the need for chain sharpening with conventional sharpening tools, but these special chains do not generally last as long as other types simply because they tend to get ground down more quickly by the sharpening device.

Although there are four different types of saw chain cutter designs, all cutters can be divided into various parts. For example, each cutter has a *top plate* and a *side plate* which must be sharpened on a regular basis to keep the overall performance of the saw chain at top efficiency. The outside surface of each top and side plate is most commonly given a hard chrome finish to help keep it sharp longer.

While there are differences in cutter teeth design, the other parts of a saw chain are fairly standard. The parts that make up a typical saw chain are shown in Fig. 7-13. The center link, or drive link, of the chain hooks into the sprocket (on the side of the engine) so that the chain can be driven around the bar. In addition, the chain will also have right and left hand cutters. These cutters have a top plate that is sharpened to a fine edge for cutting. The side plate cutter releases the wood on the side while the top plate chips wood out of the middle, much like a wood chisel. The depth gauge determines how deep the top plate penetrates into the wood each time it cuts a chip.

LUBRICATION

The most important fact to remember about saw chains is that you can never over-oil a chain. The secret of long life for a saw chain is to make sure there is always plenty of oil being applied to the chain. This means also the bar and grooves of the bar. Since almost every new chain saw will have an automatic oiling device, many do-it-yourself wood cutters feel that lub-

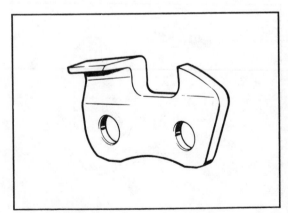

Fig. 7-12. Auto-sharp tooth.

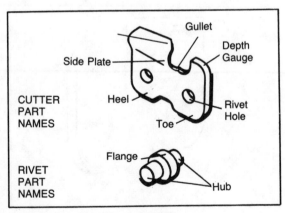

Fig. 7-13. The parts of a chain tooth.

rication is pretty much unnecessary; the device will take care of the lubrication. This is the beginning of the demise of a good chain. In addition to an automatic oiling device, most chain saws also have a manual oiler. On the better saw designs this manual oiler will be very close to the trigger and very convenient to use. Just in case you are a bit unsure as to when lubrication should be applied, let's briefly examine how and when to properly oil a saw chain.

Before you even start up your chain saw for a cutting project or task you should check to see that the lubricating oil reservoir is full of chain oil. The fuel and lubricating oil levels can be checked quickly. Top up the oil tank if required. Then, before starting your saw, give the manual oiler a few pumps and check to see that some oil is, in fact, being pumped onto the chain. In most cases, oil will be released just inside the chain cover housing on your saw, so look in this area for fresh oil after pumping.

After you have your saw running, give a few more manual pumps of oil before starting any cutting. Do this with the saw idling. Then when you pull the accelerator trigger, you should see some oil fly off the end of the chain as it passes over the tip. This is a very real indication that you are getting lubrication to the chain.

As you use your chain saw, you should periodically give the chain a few pumps of oil. This is especially important when you are about to cut large diameter logs or timber, as this type of cutting puts a good deal of strain on both the bar and chain. It is important to remember that a well-lubricated saw chain will run cooler because there will be less friction between the bottoms of the side links and cut-

ters and the rails of the bar. It will last a long time because there will be less elongation of the center link rivet holes caused by friction of the rivets. The elongation of the center link rivet holes causes the chain to "stretch" or grow longer and go out of pitch with the sprocket. As you can well imagine, chain wear or stretch can quickly ruin a chain (Fig. 7-14).

With all of this talk about how and when to lubricate a saw chain, this may be a good time to talk a bit about what type of oil to use for saw chain lubrication. Generally speaking, any oil that is specifically labeled "Chain Oil" is suitable for your chain saw (Fig. 7-15). Probably the worst choice of a lubricating oil is motor oil for it does not have the additives that bar and chain oil do to make it stick to the moving parts of the cutting system.

There have been a number of synthetic lubricants introduced over the past few years and many people have asked me if any of these are suitable for lubricating a saw chain. The answer is a *qualified* yes. The only other lubricant I recommend for saw chains is one called Tri-Flon (Fig. 7-16). I have been using this particular spray lubricant (in addition to standard bar and chain oil) for several years and

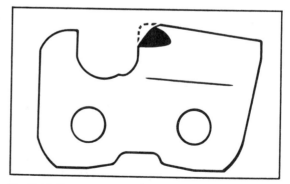

Fig. 7-14. Damaged cutter top.

Fig. 7-15. Soak a chain in oil when not in use.

have noticed that a few second spray to a moving chain will help to reduce heat and help my chain to last longer. The manufacturer recommends that a 30 second spray of Tri-Flon is the equivalent of ½ pint of conventional lubricating oil. While this may be true, I still rely on bar and chain oil for most of my lubricating. Whenever I fill the oil reservoir on my saw, I give the bar and chain a few seconds worth of spray. Personally, I think that the combination of synthetic lubricant and conventional bar and chain oil is worth the extra effort and expense. A rough estimate is that my chains stay cooler and require *half* the sharpening than if I used conventional lubricants only. You might want to try this yourself.

ADJUSTING CHAIN TENSION

A saw chain that is set at the proper tension will cut faster and more efficiently than one with excess slack in the loop. Your chain will also last longer because wear will be at a minimum. A loose chain, on the other hand, gives a slow, rough cut which has a tendency to dull the cutter teeth of your saw chain. In addition, slackness in a chain hastens sprocket tooth, chain, and guide bar wear. A chain that is too tight can cause a number of other serious and costly problems as well, so it will be to your definite advantage to learn how to properly set the tension of your saw chain.

It is important to check the tension on your saw chain before any cutting operation. To do this, first make certain that the ignition switch is in the OFF position. Then, with a suitably thick pair of gloves on your hands, try to pick the chain up off the bar. A properly adjusted chain will come up off the guide bar just a little distance (Fig. 7-17). An incorrectly adjusted chain will not budge (if too tight) or will come high enough off the bar to expose the drive link hooks (if too loose). If you feel that your chain tension is wrong, check your owner's manual for directions about how to achieve the correct tension. One word of caution when testing your chain tension is that you should never touch the chain without a pair of heavy leather gloves on your hands, for even a dull chain can cut you quickly.

Although there may be slight differences between manufacturers, all chain saws are adjusted for chain tension in about the same manner. Begin by resting the chain saw in such a way that the tip of the bar is supported on some solid object. Next, loosen the nuts on the side of the chain cover case. These lock the bar in

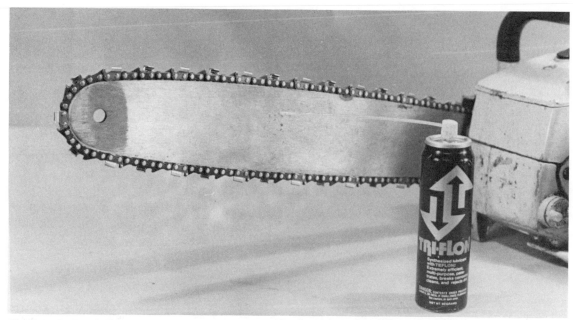

Fig. 7-16. Tri-Flon is one of the best chain lubricants to use in conjuction with chain and bar oil.

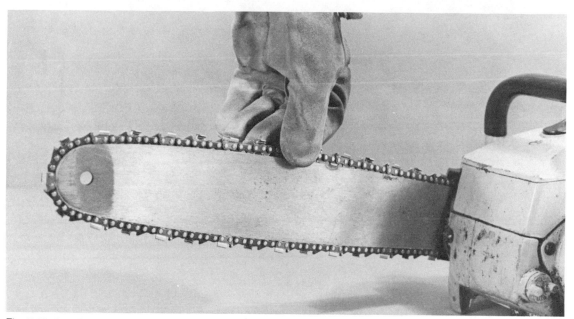

Fig. 7-17. A well-tightened chain should lift only slightly off the bar.

place, so unless you loosen them, you will not be able to move the bar. With a screwdriver or special adjusting tool, turn the adjustment screw to adjust the chain tension (Fig. 7-18). In almost all cases, turning the adjustment screw clockwise will move the bar forward, adding tension to the chain. A counterclockwise turn of the adjusting screw will move the bar towards the saw and reduce the tension on the chain. Generally speaking, a chain has the proper tension when, with the bar locked in the uppermost position, it has a snug fit all around the bar and will pull around the bar easily by (suitably gloved) hand. It is important to re-member that no droop or sag is permissible. Once you are satisfied with the tension on your chain, you can then tighten the two chain cover nuts and the saw will be ready for the cutting task at hand (Fig. 7-19).

WHEN TO SHARPEN A CHAIN

While proper lubrication and tension are very important to maintaining the life of the saw's chain, keeping the cutters sharpened and correctly filed is the most obvious way to in-crease the cutting load capacity and lifespan of the saw. But how do you know when your saw is dull or not at maximum sharpness? There are

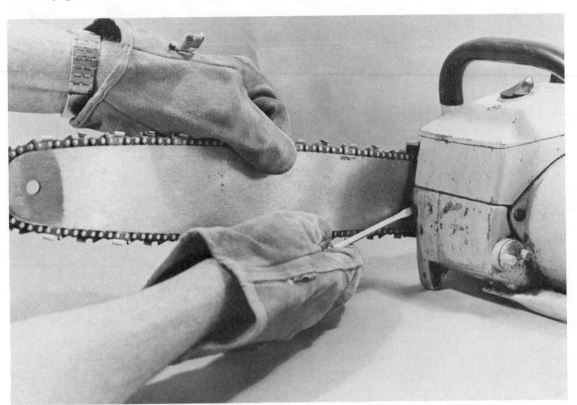

Fig. 7-18. Adjust chain tension with a screwdriver.

a number of very good indicators that you should always watch for when using a chain saw.

A sharp chain will produce solid, uniform chips, so one of the first indications that your chain is a bit dull is the presence of fine sawdust rather than chips when cutting. Another sure sign that your chain is dull is when the saw begins to cut slowly. When you find it necessary to bear down on the saw during cutting this means that the cutters are not very sharp. One last indication that your chain needs sharpening is when the chain saw will not cut straight but wants to slice right or left. If any of these conditions is present, it is probably time to sharpen (or, at the very least, touch up the teeth on) your saw chain.

SAW CHAIN SHARPENING

Before you start to sharpen your dull chain, you should first identify the size of the cutters on your chain for this will have direct bearing on the size of file to use for the sharpening. Generally speaking, there are three different size cutters in popular use today. These are listed below with corresponding file sizes (Fig. 7-20).

Fig. 7-19. A clean chain saw is a good chain saw.

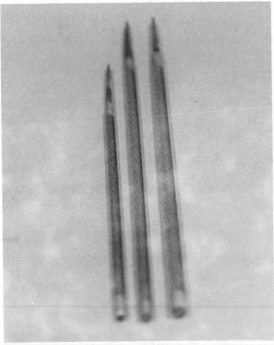

Fig. 7-20. Different diameter files are used for different size tooth chains.

Chain Cutter Size	File Size
¼ inch (6.35 mm)	5/32 inch
.325 inch (4.8 mm)	3/16 inch
⅜ inch (9.32 mm)	7/32 inch
.404 inch (10.26 mm)	7/32 inch

Once you have determined the size file required for the sharpening, and have found a suitable size wooden or plastic handle to fit it, set it aside for a few minutes until you have inspected your chain. This inspection, which can be done with the chain on the saw, is necessary to help you determine the general condition of your saw chain.

Before you begin sharpening any chain, examine it very closely and replace any broken parts (as we will describe later in this chapter). Sometimes when the cutters hit hard objects, such as stone, nails, etc., or when they cut dirt, sand, etc., the tooth will be damaged and will require that this damage be filed away before the tooth will cut or have the proper set. If one or more of the cutters have been damaged to the point of needing filing, then all of the cutters on the chain must be filed back to that same length (Fig. 7-21). The shortest cutter on the chain should serve as a guide when filing the others. To find the shortest cutter, measure the lengths of the top plate. The shorter the length of the top plate, the shorter the height of the cutter. While this filing back of all the top plates can be done by hand, it is usually less expensive (from a time standpoint) and far easier to have the work done on an electric grinder by your qualified chain saw dealer. Frequently, when only one or two cutters are shorter, it is easier to remove and replace them than file all of the cutters down to this lower level.

During your inspection of the chain, keep in mind that almost all chain problems are

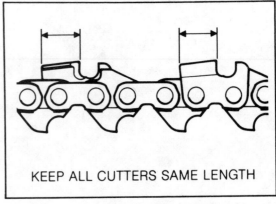

KEEP ALL CUTTERS SAME LENGTH

Fig. 7-21. Keep all cutters the same size and height.

caused by one or more of the following three things: lack of lubrication; loose chain tension; or improper filing of the cutter or depth gauge teeth.

Once you have determined what needs to be done to your chain, you can begin the actual sharpening. Of importance are the dimensions and angles of various brands and types of chains. Since these may vary somewhat, it is always best to consult your chain saw owner's manual to learn the exact filing angles required for your chain. In general, a top plate angle of from 30 to 35 degrees will render the best overall performance of the saw and chain in most types of wood. The side plate may vary anywhere from about 75 to 90 degrees, depending on the basic design of the chain in hand. The 60 degree filing angle at the top edge comes about automatically as you sharpen the top and side plates at their proper setting.

A few people can touch up a dull chain with just a file, it is better for most of us to use some kind of guide for the file when sharpening. When using a file guide, hold it flush against the top plate on the cutter so the file is parallel to the top plate. The only exception to this rule is when you are sharpening a round filed chisel type tooth, where the file angle should be about ten degrees below parallel. For all other types of chains, the file guide automatically keeps ten percent of the file diameter above the tooth. Line up the guide mark on the holder with the centerline of the chain and steady the saw's guide bar so it will not move as the filing stroke is made. Then hold the file at the correct top filing angle (for the type of chain being sharpened) and apply pressure against the cutter, pushing the file towards the front outside corner of the tooth, while at the same time

giving a slight twisting or rotating action to the file. Remember that filing should only be done on the forward stroke; move the file away from the tooth face on the return stroke.

Keep filing until the tooth is sharp, using only light but firm pressure, mostly towards the back of the tooth. For most touch-up type filing, only a few strokes will be required to sharpen each tooth. During the sharpening it is important that the file is held at the same angle. Do not dip or rock the file as this will obviously change the angle of the sharpening.

After you have sharpened one tooth, move on to the next, sharpening all teeth on one side of the chain before sharpening the others. Sharpen all left-hand cutters, for example, first; then turn the saw around and sharpen all the right-hand cutters. This approach will help you to maintain the proper angle of sharpening. As mentioned earlier, you will only have to give a few strokes of the file to touch up cutter teeth. If, for example, it takes about four strokes to sharpen one tooth, you can reasonably expect that all other teeth on the chain will also require about four strokes to sharpen. This is an important point that is easy to overlook. Just keep in mind that if you file some teeth more than others—say ten strokes rather than five—you will cause some cutter teeth to be higher or lower than the others and the end result will be a chain that does not cut well. Actually, this is one of the more difficult aspects of chain filing, since most people find it easier to file in one direction, ending up with the cutters longer on one side of the chain.

The above description of how to sharpen a saw chain will generally be enough to touch up your chain prior to or during a cutting operation. In addition to sharpening the cutter teeth of your chain, you must also file the depth gauges. As a rule, you should file the depth gauges every second or third time you touch up or sharpen the cutter teeth of your chain. As you may recall, depth gauges control the size of the chips that the cutters can cut. A tooth with a high gauge setting can obviously not take a very deep bite, and this will mean that you will be bearing down on your saw in an effort to make it cut. On the other side of the coin, depth gauges that are too low will cause the cutters to take huge bites, resulting in much jerking and bucking of the saw during a cutting operation. As you can well imagine, it is a wise practice to keep your depth gauges at the right height.

The depth at which you should keep the gauges depends upon the type of chain and the type of wood you mainly cut. The depth settings usually vary between 0.025 and 0.035 inches (0.06 and 0.09 cm) for most cutters, but check the manufacturer's recommendations for the exact setting. To make filing depth gauges easier you should pick up a special depth gauge tool (Fig. 7-22). There are a number of these inexpensive tools currently available almost anywhere chain saw equipment is sold. A tool of this type fits over your chain and covers two cutter teeth at the same time. The depth gauge of the first cutter protrudes through the guide so you can readily see how much of the guide needs to be filed off.

Depth gauges are filed with a flat file, removing only that portion of the gauge which protrudes above the special guide tool (Fig. 7-23). When filing, you must take care not to hit the cutters or other parts of the chain. Work on filing one depth gauge at a time, then move on to the next. After all of the depth gauges have been lowered, you must then go back and round off the leading edge on each depth gauge. It is important that you maintain the same profile as the original depth gauge. One tip worth mentioning is to always place the depth gauge to be filed at the same place on the guide bar. Remember that depth gauges do no cutting but do have a bearing on how much bite the cutter teeth will take.

Whenever you adjust the depth gauges on a saw chain (every two or three sharpenings) you should also examine the drive tangs or links as well (Fig. 7-24). Chain drive links must have sharp points to clean sawdust from the guide bar groove and the bar groove must be deep enough all the way around the guide bar. If necessary, clean, clear, and lightly resharpen the drive tang with a small round file to restore the cleaning hook. Be sure to maintain the precise original shape of the tangs.

CHAIN SHARPENING AIDS

If you wander into any store which has chain saws and related equipment, you are bound to see any number of sharpening devices that are aimed at the chain saw user. Since

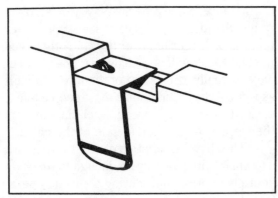

Fig. 7-22. Depth gauge.

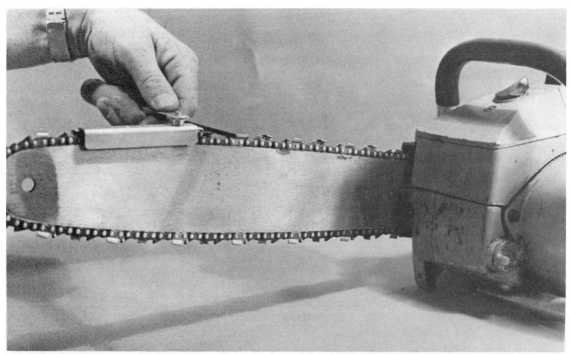

Fig. 7-23. Depth gauge in use with flat file.

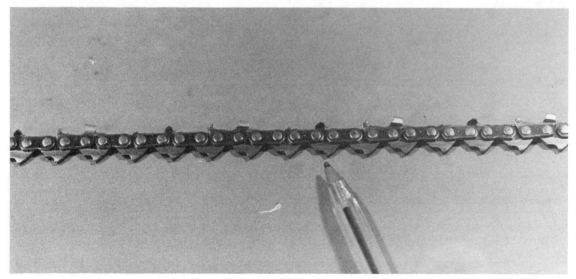

Fig. 7-24. Check the drive tangs of your chain for signs of wear.

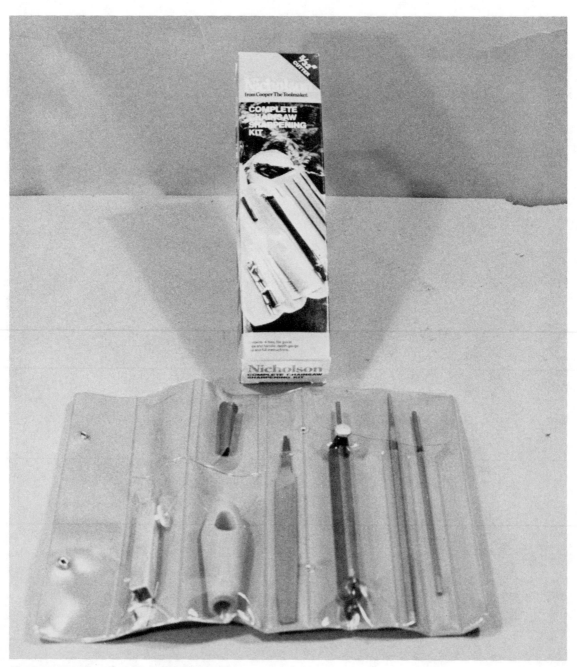

Fig. 7-25. Nicholson Chain Saw Sharpening Kit.

many of these gadgets are worthwhile, this may be a good time to explain the value of several. These are designed to make chain sharpening easy by taking as much of the guesswork as possible out of the task. Some aids are simply a file holder which has special markings to guide you in the proper angle of filing. One good example of this type of sharpening aid is available in the Nicholson Complete Chainsaw Sharpening Kit (Figs. 7-25, 7-26).

The Nicholson Kit is an inexpensive and handy addition to your woodcutting equipment.

There are three different size kits available (7/32, 5/32, and 1/8 inch file sizes) for the three most popular saw chain sizes. Each kit contains three round files (of the same diameter) for sharpening your chain, one flat mill bastard file (for planing the depth gauges), one depth gauge tool (with special inserts that enable you to use this one depth gauge for all saw chains), file handle, and a round file holder with markings to indicate the proper filing angle. The kit comes wrapped up in a handy plastic wallet which makes it very compact and easy to carry around. Nicholson also includes helpful

Fig. 7-26. Nicholson Chain Saw Sharpening Kit is very compact.

sharpening instructions in the kit to make filing a saw chain fairly easy to accomplish. Part of the real beauty of this particular chain saw sharpening kit is that there are not any attachments which must be secured to the bar of your saw before using. The end result is a sharpening kit that is easy and fast to use for touching up a slightly dull chain—the type of chain you are most likely to encounter while cutting firewood.

The Granberg File-N-Joint (Fig. 7-27) is a more sophisticated bar-mounted chain saw sharpening device than the Nicholson Kit described above. Generally speaking, the File-N-Joint is a fast, lightweight, precision tool

that sharpens chain teeth and adjusts depth gauges on all makes, sizes, and kinds of saw chain from ¼ to ½ inch pitch chain. It has short chain clamps for fast setup and a hinged chain stop for feather-light action. A lower silhouette matches modern, lower saw chains; a new dogleg file holder takes six and eight inch long files from ⅛ to ¼ inch in diameter, as well as normal flat mill bastard depth gauge jointing files. In addition, the Granberg File-N-Joint has a handled, adjustable file holder which permits the use of the full length of a file. The File-N-Joint is almost infinitely adjustable so it is adaptable for any saw chain you may come up against. It is ideal for putting a uniform, sharp

Fig. 7-27. File-N-Joint chain saw sharpening device is very handy.

Fig. 7-28. The Dremel Chainsaver in use.

cutting edge on every tooth in the chain and is therefore a worthwhile tool to have. While the Granberg File-N-Joint can be used in the field, in my opinion it is best suited for workshop use.

The next chain saw sharpening device that I think is worthwhile is the Dremel Chainsaver. This little unit is an electrically-powered hand-held sharpener that is suitable (with proper size grinding stone) for all popular saw chain sizes (Fig. 7-28). Generally speaking, the Dremel Chainsaver is as good as a professional sharpening service, if the user keeps a keen eye on the grinding. Because it is electrically-powered, the Chainsaver can re-move metal from the cutting edge of a chain tooth quickly, and it is extremely important that the user give undivided attention during the task. Complete instructions are included with each unit and offer much information about balancing the grinding stone and adjusting the grinding guide for most effective sharpening. At the time of this writing. Dremel only offers this sharpener for house current operation but I am told that a future model will be suitable for field sharpening. This new version will be powered by 12 volt direct current as from an automobile electrical system (Figs. 7-37, 7-38).

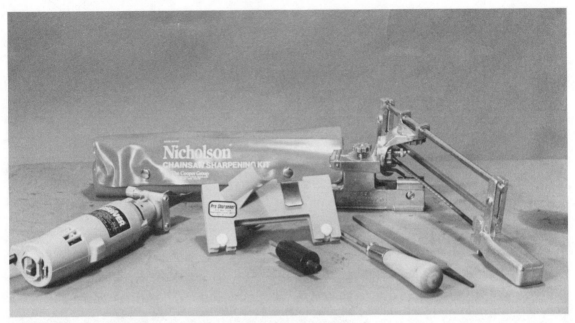
Fig. 7-29. There are many types of chain saw sharpening kits available.

To be sure, there are other chain saw sharpening kits available and new versions spring up every fall (Fig. 7-29). The important thing to remember is that a sharp chain is the *only* type you should use and chances are good that a special sharpening kit or electrically-powered tool will help you to achieve that end. As you become more experienced at sharpening, you will probably be able to keep your saw chain sharp with a suitable file as your main sharpening aid (Fig. 7-30). This is especially true for light touch-up sharpenings which are commonly done in the field.

If you are a little apprehensive about ready-made kits, as most handymen are, you will be more inclined toward making up your own chain saw sharpening kit—personalized maintenance kit that you can carry into the field along with your chain saw. I have been using such a kit for several years now and I would like to offer you a peek inside at a number of handy items. Probably the best approach for this is to simply list the items that I have in my chain saw work box. You can use your own imagination as to the purpose of the tools. I should point out that this particular kit goes with me when I use a chain saw and I have always been able to remedy common problems as they crop up (Fig. 7-31).

☐ Assortment of round and flat files.

☐ Filing guides (both clamp-on and hand-held).

☐ File handles.

☐ Depth gauge.

☐ Bar wrenches—7/16 and ½ inch.

☐ Screwdrivers—SAE and Phillips #2.

☐ Spark plug wrench.

☐ New or clean spark plug.

Fig. 7-30. File with guide is useful for touching up a dull chain in the field.

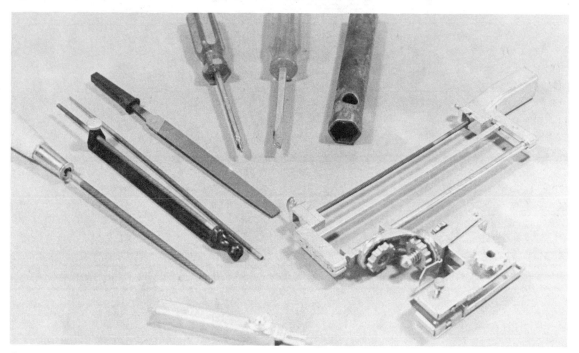

Fig. 7-31. A good chain saw sharpening collection.

☐ Set of feeler gauges.
☐ Needle-nose pliers.
☐ Vise-Grips.
☐ Grease gun for roller nose bar.
☐ Spray silicone—WD-40 or Tri-Flon.
☐ Chain and bar oil.
☐ 2-cycle oil and gasoline, mixed.
☐ Small funnel.
☐ Clean cloth rags.

☐ Long-handled ax.
☐ Splitting mall—5 lb.
☐ Wedge.
☐ 50 feet of 9mm braded nylon rope.
☐ 2 D-rings, for climbers.
☐ Small snatch block.
☐ 10 feet climbing harness belt material.
☐ Goggles.
☐ Gloves.
☐ Log lifter or cant hook.

In addition to the above chain saw service tools and parts, I also have a woodcutting box which contains a number of handy tools for this task. In the interest of providing you with another handy batch of gear to carry around, I will list these items as well (Fig. 7-32).

The above list of woodcutting equipment should provide you with all of the necessary tools for cutting and handling firewood in the field. One other addition worth considering is a sawbuck. This aid, though somewhat cumber-

Fig. 7-32. Some handy tools for wood gathering.

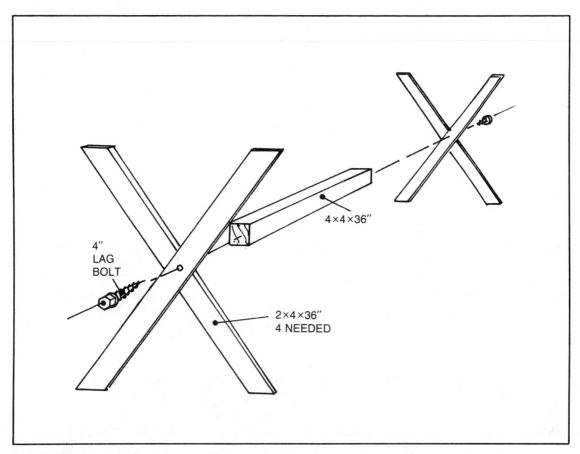

4" LAG BOLT

4×4×36"

2×4×36"
4 NEEDED

Fig. 7-33. Plan for sawbuck.

some, can be used in the field or around your home woodpile.

Since a chain saw must be held with two hands, one of the most difficult tasks in cutting firewood (assuming that you work alone) is to hold the log in a fixed position while cutting. A sawbuck is one of the best solutions to this problem. It will not only hold a log for you but will also save you some back strain, since you will be working at waist height rather than on the ground. In addition, a sawbuck will also save some wear and tear on your chain as the chances of cutting earth or rocks (as is often the case when working on the ground) is totally eliminated.

To be effective, a well-made sawbuck must be sturdy as it will receive some punishment during use. Logs tend to be thrown on, rather than carefully placed. Other than this one requirement, you are pretty much on your own when building a sawbuck. Generally speaking, the traditional sawbuck consists of two wooden Xs connected together by one or two horizontal pieces of log or lumber. Use lag bolts, nuts and bolts, or long spikes to hold the pieces together. Figure 7-33 can be used as a general guideline for constructing your own sawbuck.

GUIDE BAR AND SPROCKET

While almost all problems with your chain saw guide bar can be directly attributed to a poorly-maintained saw chain, you should nevertheless do several things to your guide bar periodically to ensure its long life. You should know at this point that incorrect filing of saw chain (either cutter or depth gauge) will cause your guide bar to wear unevenly. This uneven wear will cause a batch of problems such as uneven cutting, widening of the guide bar slots, chain clatter, and, in the more advanced stages, connecting rivet popping.

Chain tension also plays an important role in the life of your guide bar. A properly tensioned saw chain will not cause any appreciable wear to the guide bar—assuming, of course, that adequate lubrication is always present. A chain that is too tight on the other hand will cause the tip of the guide bar to wear excessively. A saw chain that is too loose will cause uneven wear on the bottom edge of the guide bar and will also contribute to excessive wear to the sprocket. In most cases it is possible to avoid a myriad of problems by properly adjusting the tension on your saw chain, keeping the cutters and depth gauge in top condition, and providing sufficient lubrication at all times. Since all of these tasks were covered earlier in this chapter we will not dwell on them here. Instead, we will turn our attention to looking for signs of problems on the guide bar and sprocket and offer suggestions for correcting these before they reach advanced stages where often the only solution is replacement of the bar and/or sprocket.

To be effective, the guide bar rails should be square and flat. To check the squareness of your guide bar, remove it from the chain saw and set it on a flat surface, vertically. When viewed from the end, the bar should be perpendicular to the flat surface. It is important to check both the top and bottom of the guide bar for squareness. If the guide bar leans to one side or the other, one of the rails on the bar is worn excessively (Fig. 7-34).

Another effective test for checking the condition of your chain saw guide bar involves the use of a straight edge. A carpenter's square works well for this test. With the chain still on the bar and properly tensioned, place the straight edge against the side of the guide bar and one cutter (Fig. 7-35). If there is clearance between the edge of the bar and straight edge, it is safe to assume that the guide bar is in good condition. If, however, the chain leans away from the straight edge and there is no clearance between the side of the bar and straight edge, the guide bar rails are worn excessively. If the latter is the case, then the bar must be reground or replaced as required.

With the guide bar removed from your chain saw there are a number of things that you should look for (Fig. 7-36). A careful inspection will often reveal areas that seem to be worn more than others. This is especially true around the area where the guide bar is fastened to the body of the chain saw. You should also look for blue spots, which indicate a pinched rail and excessive heat; broken or chipped sections; and a loose or excessively-worn sprocket nose (if your guide bar is so equipped).

In most cases, early detection of guide bar problems is the best way of prolonging the life of your bar. As soon as a problem is discovered, it can then be corrected before it gets to an advanced stage. On the other hand, problems that go undetected or are not repaired

Fig. 7-34. Lay guide bar on a flat surface to check that it is flat and not warped.

Fig. 7-35. Use a tri-square to check your guide bar.

Fig. 7-36. Look over your guide bar carefully for signs of trouble.

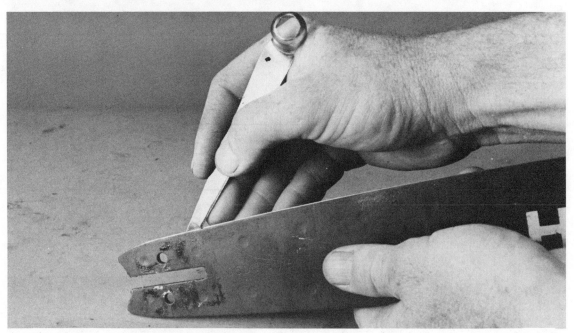

Fig. 7-37. Clean the chain guide slots on the bar often.

quickly often result in added expense as more often than not the only solution will be to replace the guide bar in its entirety.

Just because your guide bar is in good condition does not mean that it doesn't require some attention. Periodically—say after every ten or so hours of use—you should remove your guide bar and carefully inspect it for problem signs. While doing this you should also clean out the bar groove. This is not easily accomplished with a suitable tool or implement such as a piece of wire, blade of a pocketknife, stiff wire brush, etc. (Fig. 7-37). You should also check and clear the oiler hole at the back end of the bar at this time as well (Fig. 7-38). If you have a sprocket tip on the guide bar, this should also be lubricated—most commonly with a pressure grease gun. When you reinstall

the guide bar on the chain saw, turn the bar over to equalize the wear on the bar grooves. This single act alone will double the life of your guide bar under most normal conditions.

Since most modern chain saws now have a special sprocket or roller tip at the end of the guide bar, it will be helpful to explain some necessary facts at this time. Generally speaking, a roller tip extends the life of a guide bar because traditionally most of the wear is on this area of the guide bar. A roller tip guide bar should last for a long time if it is kept lubricated sufficiently. This task is best accomplished with a special pressure grease gun and should be done at least every time you fill the gas and oil tanks (Fig. 7-39). Under especially extreme conditions—such as cutting dry or highly abrasive woods, making boring cuts (with the tip of

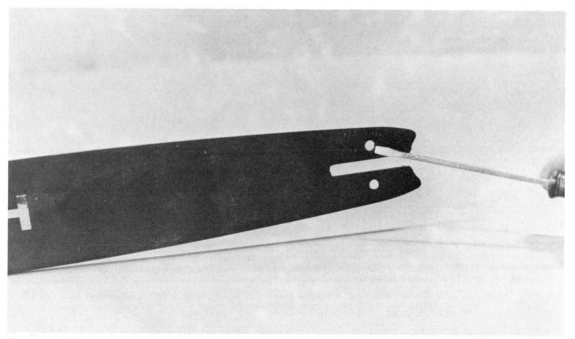

Fig. 7-38. Make certain that the oil holes are clear.

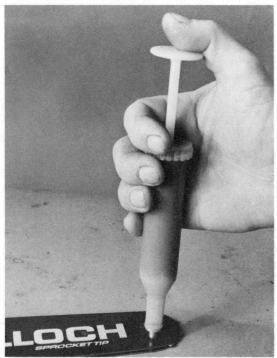

Fig. 7-39. All sprocket tip guide bars require lubrication regularly.

the saw), and cutting in snowy or wet conditions—the bar tip should be regreased after about every half tank of fuel. When lubricating, it is important to use a good grade of lithium-bearing grease, as this is the longest lasting.

Eventually even the best cared-for sprocket tip guide bar will require a new tip. One real indication of this is when lubrication does not make the sprocket turn easy. While there is nothing particularly difficult about replacing a sprocket tip, the task will require a little skill and careful attention. For those of you who feel fairly qualified, here's how best to accomplish the change.

Begin by carefully drilling off the heads of the rivets which hold the sprocket tip in place. Next, punch out the remainder of the rivets, remove the old sprocket, and thoroughly clean the tip area of the bar. To install a new sprocket (suitably sized from the manufacturer), simply slip the new roller in place until the rivet holes line up with the holes in the end of the guide bar. Then install the new rivets supplied with the replacement tip and gently peen them in place. Exercise care when peening the rivets, making certain that you do not hit the guide bar body. After the new tip is in place, it must be greased before use. This is best accomplished with a special grease gun filled with a good grade lithium-bearing grease. Pump grease into the filler hole until grease comes out of the end of the tip. If, during the removal of the old roller tip, the nose rails were spread excessively, they may be closed by inserting the old inner race in its approximate position, then clamping the tip of the bar in a vise over the rivet area. Next, hammer the rail closed with a plastic or rawhide hammer. Never use a steel hammer for this. The last step is to reinstall the guide bar and chain on the saw.

The drive sprocket on your chain saw is a very important part as it provides the vital connection between the motor and the chain. In fact, it is what causes the chain to be carried around the guide bar. A worn drive sprocket will damage and weaken a saw chain beyond repair. If, after a careful examination of your sprocket, you find that it is worn, replace it immediately. The only cure for a worn sprocket is a new one, *period*. When you consider that a new chain costs approximately five times as much as a new drive sprocket, there is truly no economy in using a worn sprocket with a new chain.

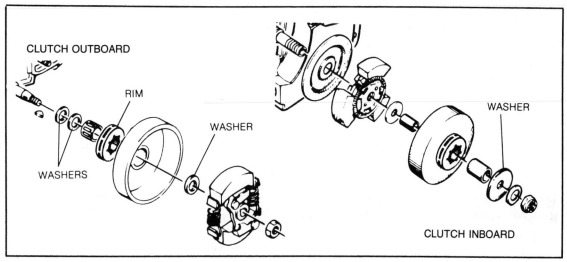

CLUTCH OUTBOARD

RIM

WASHER

WASHERS

WASHER

CLUTCH INBOARD

Fig. 7-40. The two clutch types (Oregon Saw Chain).

The best way to avoid drive sprocket problems is to check the sprocket often—whenever the chain is removed, for example. Whenever you install a new chain, chances are very good that you will also require a new sprocket as well. If you should at any time discover that your drive sprocket is wearing excessively, replace it. It is important to remember that you will get the most life out of drive sprocket if the chain is always tensioned properly. A loose chain will cause the drive links to slam into the sprocket, and an overly-tight chain will cause wear to both bar and sprocket.

Changing a drive sprocket is not a difficult task but best left to a qualified repairman if you lack the general skills and tools required for the task. Generally speaking, there are two different types of drive sprockets in use today: *clutch inboard* and *clutch outboard*. A careful examination of your drive sprocket and a comparison with Fig. 7-40 will reveal which type

you have and then you can get on with repairs. It is probably safe to say that the easier of the two installations is the clutch inboard version. Since most new drive sprockets come with complete instructions, we will not cover installation of specific drive sprockets here.

STORAGE

It is probably a safe assumption that your chain saw spends more time in storage than in actual use, unless, of course, you use this modern tool to help you earn a living. For this reason, proper storage of a chain saw should be covered at this time. It is important to know that you can add years to the life of your chain saw by storing it properly.

When storing a chain saw during the woodcutting season, all that is generally required is a cleaning of exterior surfaces with a stiff brush and clean cloth. Then give the bar and chain a liberal spray with silicone lubricant. Store the chain saw upright and away heat sources—furnace, water heater, etc.—and in as dustless an environment as possible. You should run your chain saw for a minimum of five minutes every 30 days when it is stored in this manner. If you find this is impossible to accomplish, you should store your chain saw as if for long-term storage as described next.

When storing your chain saw for long periods of time, a number of things must be done to help your saw to survive storage. You should know also that preparation for storage will also render your saw inoperable for the period of storage. The steps required for long term chain saw storage are as follows:

☐ Empty all fuel from the tank into a suitable container. Be careful as gasoline is potentially dangerous when transferring.

☐ Start the saw and let it run at idle speed until it stops, indicating that almost all of the fuel has been drawn out of the gas line and carburetor.

☐ Remove the spark plug and pour about one teaspoon full of 30 weight engine oil into the hole. Next, pull the starter cord several times so that this oil is evenly distributed in the cylinder. Then replace the spark plug tightly.

☐ Remove the chain and bar from the saw body. Wear heavy gloves and work carefully when handling chain.

☐ Place the chain in a small container—a coffee can is ideal—and cover with engine oil. Next, cover the container tightly and store in a safe place.

☐ Clean the bar with a stiff brush, then coat with a heavy film of engine oil. Then cover with heavy paper or cloth and store in a safe place.

☐ Clean all parts of the saw housing you can reach with a stiff, soft brush and cloth. While cleaning, check for any loose or missing screws, bolts, etc., and tighten or replace where required.

☐ Store your clean chain saw in the original package or other suitable box. Do not seal the box tightly or otherwise prevent air circulation of some type. Store in a safe place away from any heat source or other possible sources of combustion.

When it becomes time to use your chain saw, there are a number of things that must be done first. Begin by removing the spark plug and pulling the starter cord several times to clear the cylinder of oil. This small act will also provide a bit of needed lubrication to slightly dry parts. Next, clean and gap the spark plug and install it in the engine. Remove the wrapping from the bar and wipe it down with a cloth, then install it on the chain saw. Remove the chain from the oil bath storage and either let it hang for a few minutes to allow some of the oil to drip off or carefully wipe off the excess with a cloth. Remember to wear gloves when doing this as the chances of being cut by the sharp (and oily) teeth are great. Install the chain on the bar and tighten all connections. Next fill the fuel tank (with fresh fuel/oil mix) and oil tank. Before starting the chain saw, give the bar and chain a few seconds of silicone spray. Turn the switch on and pull the starter cord. The saw should start after a few pulls—if not, consult your owner's manual. Before any cutting takes place, run your saw for a few minutes to make certain that the automatic oiling device is working and that the saw is running well.

CHAIN SAW SAFETY

With all of the information about wood

heat and chain saws in magazines, newspapers, and even television I am a bit surprised that no more space is devoted to chain saw safety. It has been my experience that many people do not realize the power of a chain saw and, as a result, often learn that a chain saw is very dangerous to use and even to be around. Let's discuss some important safety practices that you should be aware of. Even if you are an experienced professional—a logger, for example—it may be worth your while to refresh your memory about chain saw safety.

To begin with, when you are working with a chain saw, it is important to wear the right type of clothing. A good woodcutting outfit might include, heavy work boots (hiking boots are my favorite), blue jeans or other heavy trousers, long-sleeved shirt, and jacket if the weather is not too warm. You might also consider wearing some type of hat and you should know that many chain saw companies suggest a hard hat or helmet.

There are also a few special safety items that you should wear when working with a chain saw. These include heavy leather gloves, goggles, and some type of ear or hearing protection. Most woodcutters wear gloves to protect their hands when working but I see very few people who wear eye or ear protection. Since the possibility of some type of eye damage always exists when working with a chain saw, you should protect your eyes from flying woodchips. There are a number of good, clear goggles available and if you don't presently own or use some type of eye protection, you should start *now*.

You should also protect your hearing. Noises above 80 db can result in hearing loss—both short and long-term. You should also know that even though most chain saws run quietly, they can easily attain 120 db and that opens the door to some type of hearing damage. The two best types of hearing protection you can use are tiny plugs that go into the ear and specially-designed plastic earmuff type hearing protectors. These two types of hearing protectors are inexpensive and effective against loud noises. Make one of these part of the equipment you wear when working with a chain saw.

Another piece of safety equipment that is worthwhile when working with a chain saw is a fire extinguisher. Since gasoline is highly flammable and the muffler on your chain saw gets very hot, the potential for some type of fire always exists. Be prepared. This is especially true when working around the home woodpile where there tends to be a great accumulation of sawdust and wood chips. At the very least, you should have a bucket of water or a garden hose ready to fight a small fire. If you decide to go with a conventional fire extinguisher, those rated for fighting Class A, B, and C fires are most effective. A small fire extinguisher is also very handy for carrying into the field as well.

Because a chain saw is potentially dangerous, you must exercise extreme care when working—both by yourself and around others. Keep small children out of the area unless they are being watched by a responsible person. Loud noises attract children like the Pied Piper and it is not a good idea to divide your attention between working with a chain saw and watching kids. If children are present, some type of hearing protection should be provided for them as well.

As you work with a chain saw, do not take

chances that reduce your margin of safety. For example, do not climb a tree with a chain saw. If you find it necessary to cut off limbs from a standing tree, try to accomplish this work with a handsaw. If you must use a chain saw in a standing tree, first climb up and position yourself. Then hoist up your saw with a rope. Know in advance that limbing a standing tree requires skill and experience and probably should be done only by a professional.

When cutting firewood, use a sawbuck. This will increase your margin of safety and reduce the chance of injury. A sawbuck will also reduce the chances of damaging your chain and bar. If you have someone help you with the cutting, have him (or her) stand off to your side a safe distance—loading the sawbuck, for example.

The modern chain saw is an extremely useful tool for gathering firewood and other related tasks. If used properly, this tool can make short work of big tasks. You can get the most out of this tool by keeping it sharp and in top operating condition at all times.

Chapter 8

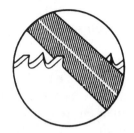

Miscellaneous Sharpening

The average American homeowner and do-it-yourselfer can easily determine that a particular tool or device requires some type of cutting (or at least dressed) edge. In some cases the need for sharpening becomes obvious (such as a wood chisel, which does a poor job when dull), but in others the need for sharpening may not be apparent at all and in fact is not even considered. Take a screwdriver, for example. Most people are surprised to learn that the tip of a screwdriver requires reshaping, especially if it is used often.

In this chapter we will take a look at a number of common tools and devices around the average home that require some type of edge treatment to keep them in tip-top shape which often translates into a useful tool. In addition, there are a number of other items used for various purposes that will benefit from

sharpening or regrinding. To be sure, the list in this chapter is not complete but it is extensive enough to give you a basis for judging if a particular item in hand will benefit from some type of edge treatment.

ALLEN WRENCHES

Allen wrenches are used for a variety of automotive and general home maintenance tasks and in some cases are the only tools that can be used to accomplish a project—removing flush set screws, for example. While Allen wrenches do not require sharpening in the true sense of the word, they will benefit from some stone or file work. This is especially true when they are used often for removing metal screws.

Allen wrenches have a tendency to develop burrs with use. As this happens, they will not fit into Allen slots in fasteners. Additionally, if a burred Allen head wrench is used to remove a plastic screw—quite common on appliances—the end result will often be damage to the screw. It is wise to check the condition of the Allen wrench before using to avoid complications.

All Allen head wrenches are made from specially tempered steel, bent over on one end to resemble the letter L. There are six parallel sides which should be perfectly equal along their entire length. If burring occurs, it is generally limited to the bottom ¼ inch of either end of the tool. The best way to remove burrs is with either a flat file or bench stone.

Begin with a careful inspection of the working tip of the Allen wrench. Use a magnifying glass or other aid if necessary. More often than not, your scrutiny will reveal tiny burrs along one or more of the flat sides. Your goal is to remove these burrs without changing the shape or the Allen wrench tip. As a rule, use only light strokes of the file or bench stone, and a few strokes as possible (Fig. 8-1). It is important that you do not file beyond the burr or you will cause one side of the Allen wrench to be unequal to the other sides. This will make the tool fit poorly and render it almost useless.

When removing the burrs on an Allen wrench, do not be tempted to use a bench grinder as this machine will remove too much metal too quickly. Use only a file or bench stone and work very carefully so the basic design of the tool remains unchanged—except, of course, for the removal of the burrs.

BOX WRENCHES

Box wrenches, like other household tools, tend to suffer with age and frequent use, generally in the form of burrs and rounded inside

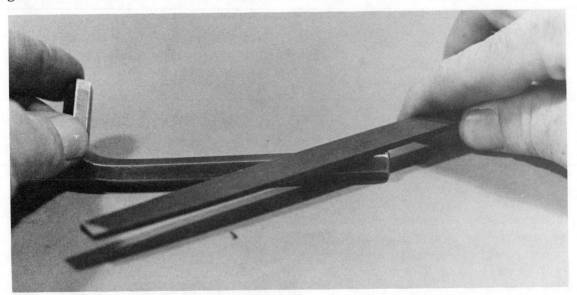

Fig. 8-1. File the ends of Allen head wrenches to remove burrs.

edges. The same things can also be said for open end and adjustable wrenches as well. For any of these tools to be effective, the inside facets must be flat, even, and free of burrs.

The best way to clean up the facets of a box wrench is with a 6-inch long slim taper file. You must work carefully with the file so the original internal shape of the wrench is not altered. Keep in mind that you are only cleaning up the metal, as it were, so that it will fit snugly over bolt and nut heads (Fig. 8-2). If too much metal is removed, the wrench will be sloppy or even useless.

The same type of treatment should be given to the open end and adjustable wrenches, except that a flat file is usually a better tool to work with. First give a few strokes to the inside of the wrench to reestablish the flatness here, then a few passes on the outside edges (Fig. 8-3). The end result should be a well-defined opening on the wrench without burrs. Here again use only enough strokes of the file to clean up the edges of the tool. If you remove too much metal, the wrench will not fit standard size nuts or bolts well and the end result will be a useless tool.

CAN OPENERS

Basically there are two different types of can openers in use today: those that make a single hole in the top of a can (a beer can opener, for example) and those that cut out the top of the can. Both types will benefit from a careful sharpening with a file or small bench stone.

Although the old "church key" type of can opener has more or less fallen by the wayside (when was the last time you opened a beverage

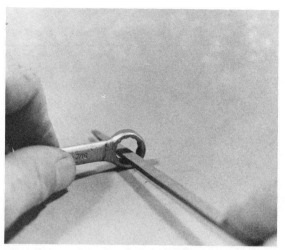

Fig. 8-2. Clean up the inside of box wrench with a slim taper file.

can that did not have a pop-top?), they are still useful for opening some types of cans around the kitchen and workshop. I keep a can opener in the garage, for example, for opening cans of crankcase and two-cycle engine oil (Fig. 8-4).

A pry-type can opener can be quickly sharpened with a flat file or by grinding. Your intention should be to reestablish the point and square off the sides of the opener, removing as little metal as possible in the process. If you use a bench grinder, do not work too long at the wheel as this will heat up the metal excessively, destroying the temper of the steel. Since a file will do the job quickly and effectively, this tool is probably the better choice for sharpening (Fig. 8-5).

Crank-type can openers are composed of two basic parts. One grabs and holds the rim of the can while the other bites through the can lid and cuts around the inside edge as the crank is turned. Some crank-type openers (Fig. 8-6) have a cutter wheel while others are simply a

Fig. 8-3. Square off the jaws of an adjustable wrench with a flat file.

piece of beveled metal. The wheel types are the most efficient and long-lived.

The easiest way to sharpen a crank-type can opener is to remove the tiny cutter wheel and hone this with a small pocket stone. Work to reestablish the original bevel all the way around the wheel. After the front bevel has been sharpened, turn the wheel over and remove the tiny wire edge that will have formed. Usually a few swipes with the stone will do this nicely (Fig. 8-7).

After sharpening a crank-type opener, give the metal parts a light coating of vegetable oil. You should also lubricate the shaft that the cutter wheel rotates on as well with the oil. Do not use any other type of oil (engine oil, for example), as this could easily contaminate the contents of a can of food. Reassemble the opener and it is ready for a trial run.

Fig. 8-4. An old "church key" still in service.

Fig. 8-5. Pry-type can openers can be quickly sharpened on a flat file.

Fig. 8-6. Crank-type can openers work well when sharp.

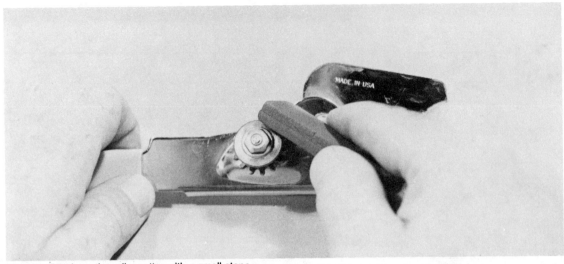

Fig. 8-7. Touch up the roller cutter with a small stone.

COLD CHISELS

Cold chisels are used for shearing off nuts and bolts, scribbing concrete-like substances, splitting logs, and similar tasks (Figs. 8-8, 8-9). Because of the nature of the work that a cold chisel is called upon to do, it takes a lot of abuse. In fact, cold chisels are *made* for being beaten upon by a sledge. For this reason it is equally necessary to condition both ends of a cold chisel—the beveled edge as well as the head.

The bench grinder is the best tool to use for conditioning a cold chisel on almost all levels. A good grinding wheel will make short work out of dressing the beveled edge, and the often mushroomed head can be trimmed quickly too. The steel that all chisels are made from tends to be heavy-duty, especially in the larger sizes, so there is little danger of heating up the metal past the temper danger point. It's always best, however, to dip the work in water to keep the overall temperature uniform.

Before you start grinding the bevel on the chisel, look over the tool carefully to see how much grinding will be required. In many cases

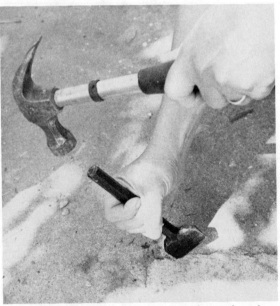

Fig. 8-8. A cold chisel is commonly used for tough work.

Fig. 8-9. A wedge will open up even the tightest log.

you will merely be recreating the bevel, but in others—where a chunk is missing, for example—you must begin by grinding the entire cutting edge off perpendicular to the handle until the damaged section has been removed (Fig. 8-10).

When grinding a bevel on a cold chisel, you should duplicate the original edge unless you have a specific chiseling project at hand they may require a special bevel. As a rule, the harder the surface the chisel will be used on, the blunter the bevel. For example, when working on steel or other hard surfaces, a bevel of about 70 degrees will be the most long-lived. Softer surfaces such as brass and copper require a 40 degree bevel. For an all-around cold chisel edge on soft surfaces, a 60 degree bevel will be most long-lived (Fig. 8-11).

After grinding the working edge of the cold chisel, turn the tool end for end and grind the top end to remove any mushrooming steel (Fig. 8-12). In the advanced stages, the edges of a mushroomed cold chisel head have a tendency to become shrapnel in the true sense of the word. Clean up this end of the tool as required, even if it means stopping the work you are doing with the tool (Fig. 8-13).

After sharpening the working end and bevelling the head of a cold chisel, the next step is to give it a light coat of oil or a spray of silicone. The tool is then ready for service. When not in use, a cold chisel should be lightly oiled to prevent rusting.

CROWBARS

The crowbar is used for a number of tasks around the home and workshop including pulling nails, prying boards, and lifting heavy

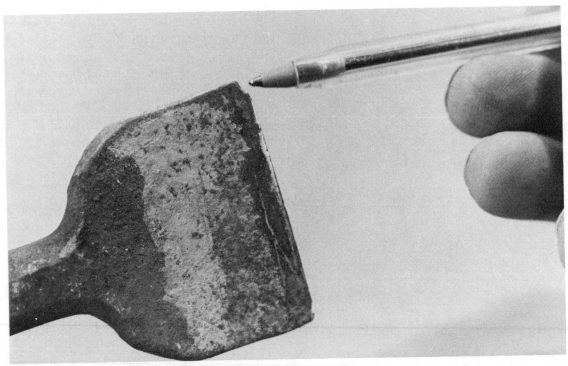

Fig. 8-10. Damaged cold chisel will require grinding.

objects a few inches. While there are a number of different designs, shapes, and sizes, all crowbars are basically the same in that they have a forked end and a flat working end (Fig. 8-14). In most cases the fork—which is used for pulling nails—will be at the curved end while the flat end is at the end of the straight shaft.

A crowbar is not sharpened in the true sense of the word but is should have well-defined edges at both ends of the tool. Often, as a result of banging a crowbar with a hammer, parts of the tool will become peened over along the shaft. If these are not ground off, they will be a constant source of cuts on your hands. The edges of a crowbar can be cleaned up, as it were, with either a file or bench grinder, de-

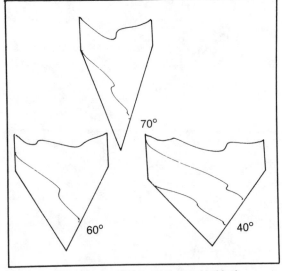

Fig. 8-11. Three bevel angles used on cold chisels.

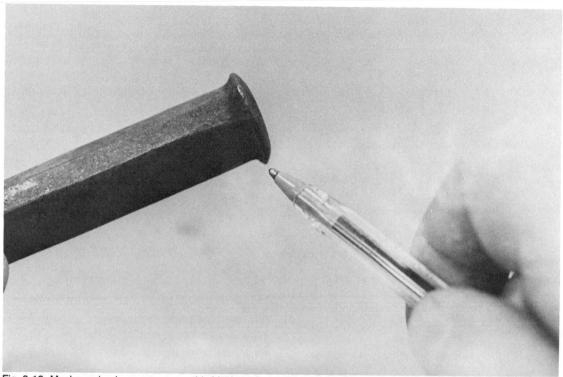

Fig. 8-12. Mushrooming is common on cold chisels and must be ground off.

pending of course on how much work is involved. When cleaning up the edges, it is important that you do not remove too much metal; this will weaken the tool and make it useless for heavy work. When cleaning up the forked end of a crowbar (the end which is commonly used for pulling nails) remove as little metal as possible or this important part of the tool will not have enough integrity to accomplish the task at hand (Fig. 8-15). Your intention is only to clean up the insides of the fork and not change the basic design of the fork.

FISHHOOKS

I think most fishermen (and women) will

Fig. 8-13. A clean cold chisel head.

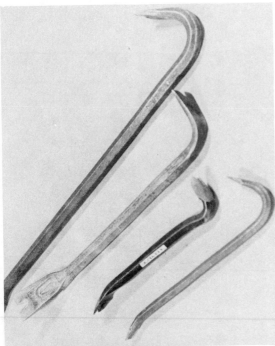

Fig. 8-14. Crowbars come in many shapes and sizes.

agree that the underlying intention of fishing is to hook a fish. This is most easily accomplished with a sharp fishhook. But did you know that once you use a fishhook it begins to dull, and the more you use it, the duller it becomes? In time, the average fishhook is so dull it will require a considerable amount of effort to set (pull into the lips or jaw of a fish) and the end result more often than not is a lost fish. If you doubt that a fishhook becomes dull, compare a fishing lure that has been in use for a season with one that is brand new (Fig. 8-16).

Every tackle box and fishing vest should contain some means of sharpening fishhooks—a small file (an ignition file is ideal) or pocket stone. Sharpen fishhooks by filing the sides of the point and the barb into a sharp wedge shape (Fig. 8-17). This way no metal is removed from the outside of the hook point. This generally means that the hook will be strong after sharpening as it was originally.

Fig. 8-15. Clean burrs in crowbar fork with slim taper file but do not remove too much metal or the tool will be weakened.

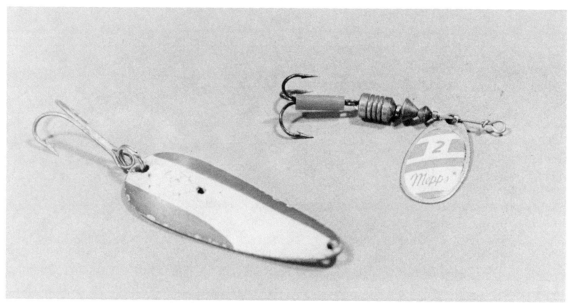

Fig. 8-16. Fishing lures need sharpening occasionally.

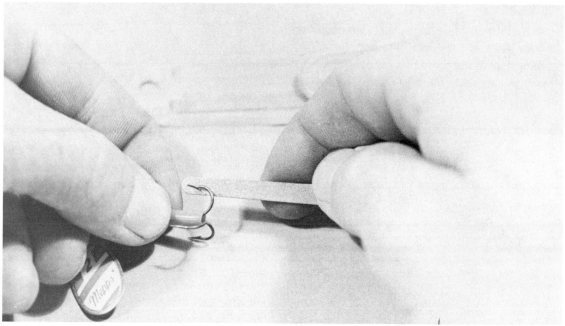

Fig. 8-17. Sharpen the barbs of a fishhook with a small file.

fishhooks must depend on how often you use a particular lure and the type of water where you fish. For example, if you fish in deep water, chances are the hook will stay reasonably sharp. But if you fish in a rocky river or stream, where the lure is often bumped along the bottom, you might want to sharpen the hook (or hooks) after a few hours of fishing. Another way fishhooks become dull is when lures are packed together in a tackle box. Lure bodies and hooks become a mass entanglement and hooks become dull. It is also common for hook points to break off when they are stored in this manner. To save yourself some work in both untangling and sharpening, store lures in individual compartments or with special hook bonnets (Fig. 8-18).

ICE PICKS

An ice pick is used for chipping off chunks from a block of ice and is often called on for making screw-starter holes. To be effective at this type of work the tip should come to a needle-like point. This type of point can be

Fig. 8-18. Special hook bonnets will protect sharp fishhooks when not in use.

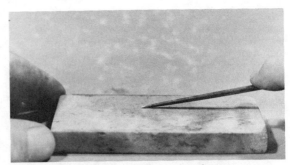

Fig. 8-19. Sharpen an ice pick on a bench stone.

easily developed with a small stone. Simply rotate the tool between your fingers while at the same time stroking it along the stone. The shaft of the pick should be lifted slightly so that the resultant point will have somewhat of a bevel. It is important, from the standpoint of durability, that the point not be a full taper but rather a taper which ends in a beveled point (Fig. 8-19).

ICE SKATES

The blades of ice skates have a tendency to mushroom slightly with age. If the skates are worn while walking over hard surfaces such as concrete, this will dull the skates as well. It is probably a good idea to look over the blades of ice skates before the season begins and put them in first-class working order.

While professional sharpening services have a special jig for holding the blade while grinding, you can achieve almost the same results with a bench stone in your own workshop. Begin by clamping one skate in a bench vise with the blade up. Next, take a fine-grained stone and stroke the bottom edge of the blade a few times while keeping the flat of the stone perpendicular to the edge. After the bottom edge has been cleaned up in this manner, take the skate out of the vise and rub the stone along both sides of the blade to remove any burrs or curls that may have formed. You should use a bit of oil when sharpening ice skates in this manner to help the stone cut and slightly polish the edges. After sharpening, remove all metal particles, and oil with a clean cloth. When not in use, the blades of ice skates should be covered to protect the edge. Special ice skate covers are available for this purpose.

SCISSORS

There is probably nothing quite as frustrating as a pair of dull scissors. They don't cut worth a darn and more often than not give a raggedy edge to the material being cut. The blades of a quality pair of scissors are not flat as they appear at first glance, but are instead concave. This design feature causes pressure to be exerted along the point of the cut as the scissors are opened and closed. This tension is further enhanced by the pivot screw.

As a rule, you should not sharpen scissors unless they are very dull. Often, simply tightening the pivot screw will give a marked improvement in how they cut, so you should try this before deciding to sharpen the edges (Fig. 8-20).

The bevel cutting edges on a good pair of scissors are at an angle of approximately 80

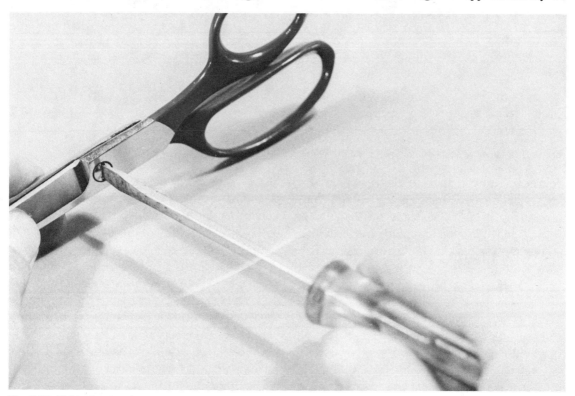

Fig. 8-20. Tightening the pivot screw on scissors will often make them cut better.

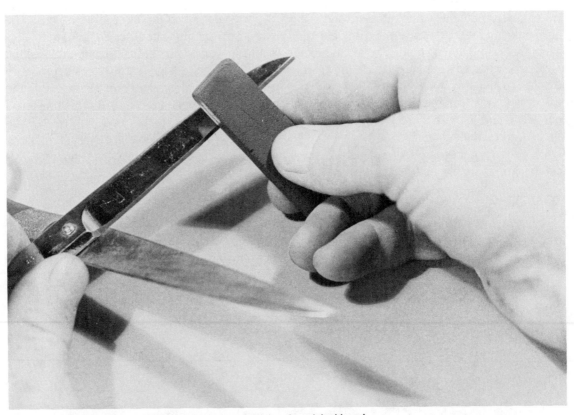
Fig. 8-21. Sharpen scissors with a small stone, maintaining the original bevel.

degrees. You can restore this easily with a fine-grained stone simply by stroking several times (Fig. 8-21). Use some oil to help the honing and give your undivided attention to recreating the bevel. The bevel must be consistent along the entire cutting edge. This will require careful work, especially for long-bladed shears. After a few swipes on each blade, clean off any oil and metal and then open and close the scissors several times. This action will remove the tiny wire edge that will have formed on the backside of the blades. The next step is to make a test cut on heavy paper. This test will reveal if the bevels are true (Fig.

8-22). A clean cut means that the sharpening was done correctly, but a ragged-edged cut means that the bevel is inconsistent. Look over both blades carefully to discover the source of the problem and correct as necessary.

Scissors can also be sharpened on a belt sander but some type of dependable tool rest should be rigged up first—not only to steady the tool, but at the desired edge bevel as well. Open the scissors as wide as they will go, then place on the edge guide. The belt should travel into the edge. Move the scissors into the belt at the proper bevel and make a quick pass. It is important that the scissors be kept in motion or

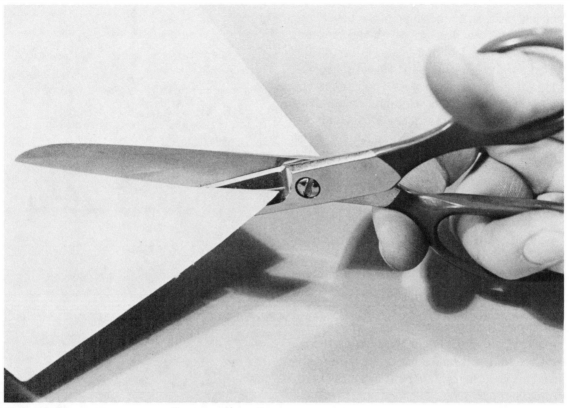

Fig. 8-22. After sharpening, make a test cut with the scissors.

a flat spot will result which will make the scissors useless. As a rule, a light touch is far better than trying to force the bevel on the sander. Grind the second blade in the same manner.

After sharpening scissors by either of the two methods described above, they should be cleaned with a dry cloth. It is important to remove any oil and metal particles from the sharpening. Next, check the tension of the pivot screw and adjust if necessary. The last step is to apply a coat of clean, lightweight oil to all surfaces of the scissors. Ten weight oil is a good choice. This lubricating oil should be

worked into the scissors by opening and closing them several times. Then take a clean dry cloth and remove all of the oil. Now the scissors are ready for service.

The general sharpening procedures outlined above will work with most types of scissors but there are some exceptions that are worth noting. If scissors have other than flat or straight cutting edges—pinking shears, for example—you must sharpen in a different manner. As a rule, special-edged scissors require a small stone for sharpening. You should sharpen only the top edges of the irregular blade and not the shear faces. Work carefully and just sharpen up the angle of the bevel with the stone. A few drops of oil should be used. After you have done the best you can on the bevel, make a few passes to the backside of the blade to remove any feather edge. Wipe the scissors clean with a dry cloth, removing all oil and metal particles, then make a test cut. If you are not satisfied with the cutting action, adjust the pivot screw and this should correct the problem.

SCREWDRIVERS

To be effective, the tip of a flat-bladed screwdriver must be square and should fit snugly into a screw slot. More often than not, when a screwing task is at hand, the first screwdriver available is the one that gets used. Just as often, the tip of the screwdriver does not fit well into the screw slot and the end results are commonly a stripped screw head, skinned knuckles, and a poor overall job. The need for choosing a proper-fitting screwdriver from the three or four that are common in most households is important for success. In addition, the tip of a screwdriver is used, the greater the chances of it becoming rounded and much less effective.

If a screwdriver becomes nicked in the tip, this damage must be repaired on the bench grinder (Fig. 8-23). Begin by adjusting the tool rest so that the end of the screwdriver can be ground off at a perfect 90 degree angle to the shaft of the tool. Do not let the screwdriver become too hot to touch or the temper of the metal will be destroyed. Keep a can of water next to the bench grinder and dip the tool into this often to keep the temperature down.

After the tip of the screwdriver has been

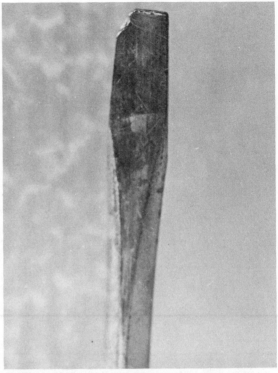

Fig. 8-23. Broken tip on screwdriver can be repaired by grinding.

squared off, the next step is to make the two flat sides of the tip parallel for about 1/16 to 1/4 of an inch. This is done by holding the screwdriver by the shank and then pressing lightly into the wheel as shown Fig. 8-24. Grind one side, then repeat the grinding in exactly the same manner on the other flat side of the tip. When you are finished, the tip should be square at end and the two flat sides should be parallel.

Phillips screwdrivers also require touching up periodically or they will jump out of a screw slot easily. The best way to clean up the tip of a Phillips screwdriver is on a bench stone

Fig. 8-24. Grind the sides of a screwdriver parallel.

(Fig. 8-25). Hold the shaft of the screwdriver at the proper bevel angle and make a few passes over the stone, while at the same time keeping the flat pressed firmly on the stone. Repeat this technique on all four flats of the tip. You should work carefully; don't remove any more metal than is required for dressing up the edge.

SPATULAS

The kitchen spatula is used for years without any thought to the leading edge. In time, however, this edge becomes rounded and thus much less effective at scraping and turning. The edge of this kitchen tool is very similar to the edge of a paint scraper or putty knife and should receive the same treatment. The leading edge should be at a perfect right angle to the blade, and the corners should be slightly rounded so it will not dig into special Teflon coatings.

The best way to dress up the edge of a spatula is with a file or bench stone. One good way to accomplish this is to clamp the tool in the jaws of a bench vise with the forward edge about ¼ inch above the jaws. Then, with a file or stone, make a few passes over the edge, lengthwise. It is important to hold the file or stone at a perfect right angle to the edge so it will be square (Fig. 8-26). Next, take the spatula out of the vise and give a few strokes to the side to remove any feathering. Lastly, round off the corners of the spatula to prevent it from digging when in use (Fig. 8-26).

If the blade of your spatula is made from thick gauge steel, you may want to bevel the bottom ¼ inch of it to help it work more efficiently. To do this, first file as indicated above, then file the top edge of the blade as shown in Fig. 8-27. An angle of about 45 degrees seems to be the best for this type of kitchen tool.

TAPS AND DIES

When you need to freshen the threads on a bolt hole, the best tool for the job is a tap—with the same diameter threads, of course. Or when you require the threads of a bolt to be crisp, a

Fig. 8-25. Sharpen the flats on a Phillips screwdriver on a bench stone.

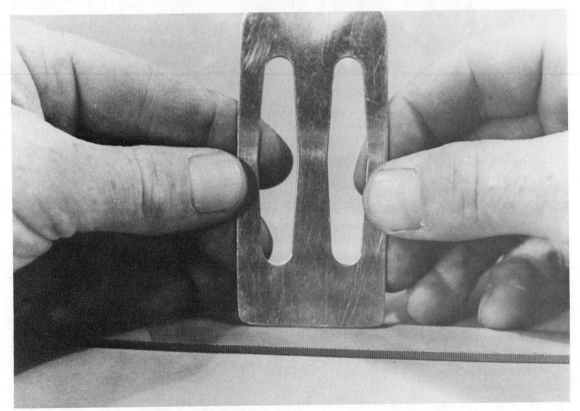

Fig. 8-26. A spatula will work better if the leading edge is square.

Fig. 8-27. For thick metal spatulas, bevel the top edge slightly.

die is the tool to choose. If you have ever worked with taps and dies, you know that the metal used for making these tools is very hard, so you may never have thought about sharpening either taps or dies. The truth of the matter is, quite simply, that taps and dies do get dull with use and will greatly benefit from a sharpening.

To sharpen a tap, you will need a small hard, fine-grained stone or a small electric grinder, such as the one used for sharpening a saw chain. The only part of a tap that can or should be sharpened is that part of the groove which is adjacent to the leading edges. When looking at a tap from the point end—the part that enters the hole first—the leading edges are those that are on the left side of each of the lands of the tool. There are four in most cases. You must work carefully with the stone so that the cutting edges are not rounded off.

When using a hand-held electric grinder fitted with a suitable size stone, you must be extremely careful as damage to the groove can happen very quickly. It is best to hold the tap firmly against a bench or in a bench vise when grinding. Work slowly and stop often to check on the progress of the work (Fig. 8-28).

When sharpening dies, you must use

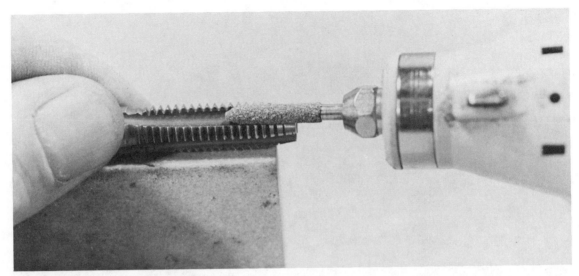

Fig. 8-28. Use a power grinder to sharpen a tap.

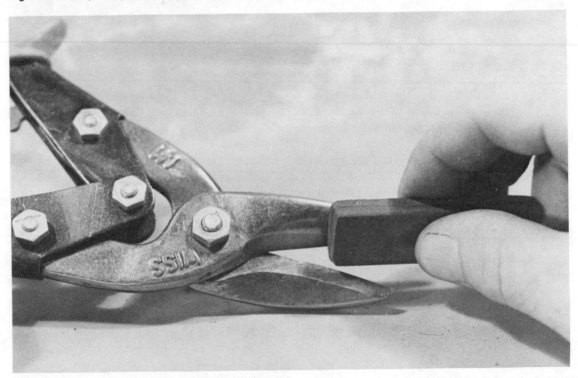

Fig. 8-29. Use a small pocket stone for sharpening tin snips.

either a small, hard, round slipstone or a hand-held electric grinder fitted with a small stone. Here again, only the groove adjacent to the leading edge is sharpened. When looking at a die from the bottom, this will be the left side of each of the lands. Work carefully so as not to round off any of the edges.

TIN SNIPS

These handy cutters have many uses around the home and workshop in addition to cutting thin sheet metal. They are strong enough for cutting canvas, leather, and other materials that are too heavy for ordinary scissors.

Tin snips can be sharpened with a stone, grinding wheel, or belt sander, but the stone is probably the best choice (Fig. 8-29). The blades on some models lend themselves to being disassembled but this is not generally necessary unless extensive grinding to remove damage is required. Simply open the snips as far as they will go and work with a stone to reestablish a crisp 25 degree angle. After both blades have been honed, whet the flat or shear faces a few times to remove any fine wire that may have developed as a result of sharpening.

After sharpening has been done to your satisfaction, you should adjust the pivot bolt or

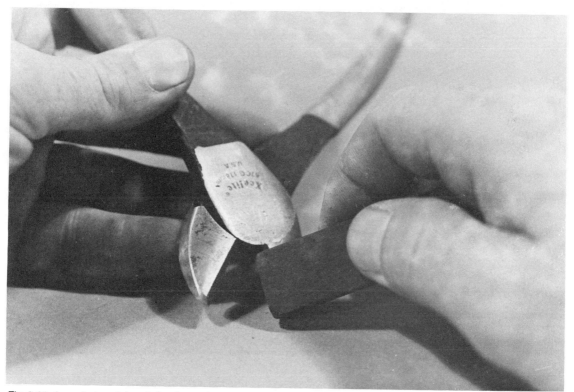

Fig. 8-30. A small stone is handy for sharpening wire cutters.

screw on the snips. This carries a heavy load when in use and proper tension is therefore important. The bolt should be tightened to the point where the shear faces are held closely but not touching. After adjusting the tension on this bolt, lubricate the area well with oil.

WIRE CUTTERS

These handy pliers are used for stripping and cutting wire of all gauges and must therefore be sharp to work effectively. A stone small enough to fit between the jaws is used for the sharpening. It is important to reestablish the original bevel, which is generally about 45 degrees. The innermost recess of the jaws usually has the least amount of wear so you should check here for the bevel angle if you are uncertain (Fig. 8-30).

Work carefully with the stone and do not remove more metal than is necessary to do the sharpening. After you are satisfied with the edges, lubricate the area around which the jaws pivot.

Index

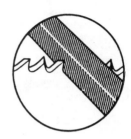

Index

Edited by Steven Mesner

About the author

Don Geary has been a professional freelance writer and photographer since 1972. A member of the Outdoor Writers Association of America and the National Association of Home & Workshop Writers, he has written over 200 articles for such magazines as *Camping Journal, Family Handyman, Organic Gardening,* and *The Mother Earth News* and was a contributing editor of *Backpacking Journal.* His published books include *The Welder's Bible, How To Design and Build Your Own Workspace*, and *The Compleat Outdoorsman*. Don's hobbies include home and kitchen rebuilding, fishing, hunting, hiking, rock climbing, and camping. Don lives with his wife and son in Salt Lake City, Utah.